The Complete Year
in Reading and Writing

Daily Lessons • Monthly Units • Yearlong Calendar

Karen McNally and Pam Allyn

NEW YORK • TORONTO • LONDON • AUCKLAND • SYDNEY
MEXICO CITY • NEW DELHI • HONG KONG • BUENOS AIRES

For all kindergarten teachers, who care so much
about the right beginnings, and:

To Chris for his love and encouragement from the very beginning.
~ *Karen McNally*

For Katie and Charlotte, whose beginnings were so joyous and
whose journeys continue to delight and astound us.
~ *Pam Allyn*

Cover design by Jay Namerow

Interior design by Maria Lilja

Photos by LitLife Archives (interior and cover), Maria Lilja (inside cover)

Acquiring Editor: Lois Bridges

Development and Production Editor: Danny Miller

Copy Editor: Erich Strom

ISBN 13: 978-0-545-04633-6

ISBN 10: 0-545-04633-5

Copyright © 2008 by LitLife Publishing LLC

All rights reserved. Published by Scholastic Inc.

Printed in the U.S.A.

2 3 4 5 6 7 8 9 10   23   13 12 11 10 09 08

Contents

As a bonus, use our Spotlight Units to journey through day-by-day
lessons in all the Complete 4 components.

Acknowledgments

We would like to thank the teachers, the children, and our colleagues in the LitLife network of schools who believe in the power of words.

There was a team of people who gave of themselves in the deepest and most generous of ways to this project. We are full of gratitude for the wise and thoughtful Delia Coppola, Janet Knight, Debbie Lera, and Michelle Yang. Their insights, feedback, and creations glow brightly throughout this series.

We are grateful for the support of our extraordinary LitLife team: the remarkable and talented Jenny Koons who understands life and people and kids and curriculum and who enriched the books with her careful eye, and the marvelous Rebekah Coleman whose spirit kept us going and whose wise attention completed us. With thanks to our dedicated interns, Jen Estrada and Alyssa McClorey, and to Deb Jurkowitz, LitLife grammarian and in-house linguist. We deeply appreciate our agent, the magical Lisa DiMona for shining the light that guides our way.

Danny Miller may very well be one of the funniest people on earth. He is also a brilliant editor. His dedicated efforts to this series are appreciated beyond compare by us all. Lois Bridges: inspiration, mentor, friend, champion of children and humanistic education, connector of all dots, editor extraordinaire, we thank you. All our appreciation to the team at Scholastic: the creative Maria Lilja, and Terry Cooper for her vision and dedication to the work of supporting teachers. In addition, we thank Eileen Hillebrand for her genius way of getting the word out there and Susan Kolwicz for her genius in getting the message heard.

This experience of writing six books together has been by turns precious, wild, funny, exhausting, scary, joyous, and deeply satisfying. We collectively gave birth to three babies during this process, visited hundreds of schools, took our own kids to school, and tried to have dinner with our husbands once in a while. From the beginning, we committed to one another that when the work felt hard we would always remember that relationships come first. We are most proud of this and hope our readers can feel the power of our bonds in every page of every book in this series. We thank one another, always.

Pam Allyn sends her boundless gratitude to Jim, Katie, and Charlotte Allyn for their love and for their countless inspirations. She would also like to thank her coauthor Karen McNally for her grace in all she does, from motherhood to friendship to work, and for her kindness to all people, big and small.

Karen McNally would like to thank those who made the writing of this book possible. To her husband, Chris, for his patience, love, and sacrifices. To her children, Jack, Kiera, and Drew for their wonderful distractions. To the many talented kindergarten teachers she has had the privilege of working with, who inspired, eagerly awaited, and cheered the early drafts of this book. To Karen's Kindergarten Leadership Team, Kim Laurie, Janet Knight, Cathy Chulla, Danielle Esposito, and Keri Fischer; remarkable teachers who piloted units, gathered work samples and took photographs for this book. Finally, Karen would like to thank her co-author Pam Allyn whose thoughtfulness, intelligence, and passion for this work know no bounds. Working on this project with her has been an honor.

Chapter 1

All About the Complete Year

Dear Kindergarten Teacher,

This is the beginning.

You dry her tears of homesickness and watch as she reaches out to her first new friend. You notice how someone packed her lunch so tenderly and later help her find her way to the bus. You are accompanying her on the beginning of her school experience; you are her mentor and her companion. She has been on this earth for just five years.

The kindergartener is looking around her world and everything is a reminder of something else. The blue color inside the fish tank reminds her of the baby blanket on her bed; the sound of laughter on the playground makes her think of her little brother. She is a traveler in a new world with longings for the old one.

Play and reflection are not separate from literacy. "Only connect," said the writer E. M. Forster. This is the work of the kindergarten child. She abides by the power of imagination. She is building worlds out of things, and things out of worlds. These are the processes by which we will foster literacy: play, imagination, and collaboration.

The imaginative life of a child is one in which any idea can fit into different containers: a couch becomes a magic ship, a pair of sneakers becomes the hooves on a horse. So, too, genre matters in the life of a kindergarten child. She wants to see herself as someone who can fit her ideas to the world. Her embrace of the sun's warmth becomes a poem. Her joy in skipping to lunch becomes a song. Her loneliness for her mother becomes a letter.

The kindergartener is already thinking strategically: How can I build this block structure? How can I make a little book? She likes to see how things get set up, how things are made. She likes to take something apart and put it back together. So, in this year, we embrace and celebrate the strategic talents of the kindergartener. She makes a book, designs a card, or puts her books together into a little basket to plan for her reading life. All of these small steps should be celebrated.

Your kindergartener is aware of language and the beauty of words themselves, keenly aware of the look of words and alphabet letters and the sounds of words. Her mind is humming with the newness of words all day long.

For your kindergartener, print represents a key to a world of older friends, of big brothers, of mother and father. She sees written language in all its glory, and she wants to be part of it, too.

Savor these days. You are in the midst of the newness of her life. And she is in the midst of yours. Together, let us unfold a year together, a year like no other: the kindergarten year.

Warmly,

Karen McNally   Pam Allyn

At-a-Glance Overview of the Complete Year

Organized around the Complete 4 components (Process, Genre, Strategy, and Conventions) and four unit stages (Immersion, Identification, Guided Practice, and Commitment), each book in the Complete Year series features a year's worth of integrated reading and writing curriculum. Because we honor your professional decision-making, you will find that the Complete Year provides a flexible framework, easily adapted to your state standards and to the needs and goals of your community, your students, and your teaching style.

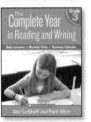
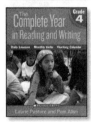
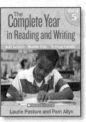

What Will You Find Inside the Complete Year Series?

Yearlong Curricular Calendar

Units of Study
- More than 25 detailed unit outlines spanning every season of the school year.
- 8 Spotlight Units including more than 100 day-by-day lessons
- 2 ARCH units to start your year right
- 2 reflective units to end your year on a powerful note

Assessment
- Individualized assessments for every unit
- Complete 4 Assessment (C4A)

Lists of Anchor Texts for Each Unit

Parent Letters

Resource Sheets and Homework Assignments

Professional Reading Lists

Glossary of Terms

DVD that features Pam Allyn sharing the benefits of the Complete 4 for the Complete Year as well as ALL downloadable assessment forms and resources. You will also find helpful links to professional development support from LitLife and easy-to-use technological support from RealeBooks to help you publish your students' work.

The Complete Year Supports...

Individual teachers wanting a clear road map and detailed lessons for reading and writing and for reading/writing connections.

School or district teams wanting to plan a continuum together with specific lessons and units that address the needs of all students—ELL, gifted, and special needs.

Administrative leaders and literacy coaches wanting to guide their school to a consistent, standards-rich plan for reading and writing instruction.

Pam Allyn's The Complete 4 for Literacy and Debbie Lera's Writing Above Standard are foundational texts for the Complete Year. LitLife and RealeBooks provide innovative professional and technological support for the Complete Year.

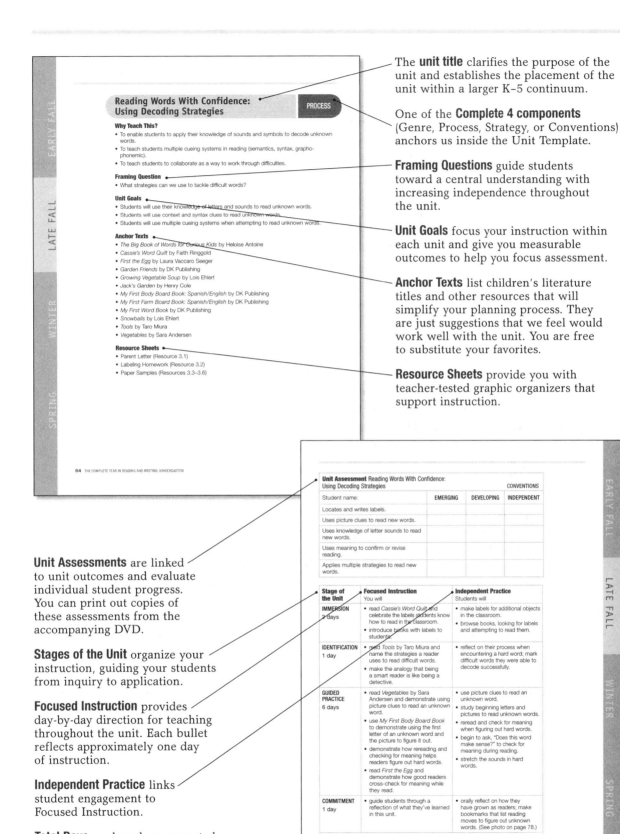

The **unit title** clarifies the purpose of the unit and establishes the placement of the unit within a larger K–5 continuum.

One of the **Complete 4 components** (Genre, Process, Strategy, or Conventions) anchors us inside the Unit Template.

Framing Questions guide students toward a central understanding with increasing independence throughout the unit.

Unit Goals focus your instruction within each unit and give you measurable outcomes to help you focus assessment.

Anchor Texts list children's literature titles and other resources that will simplify your planning process. They are just suggestions that we feel would work well with the unit. You are free to substitute your favorites.

Resource Sheets provide you with teacher-tested graphic organizers that support instruction.

Unit Assessments are linked to unit outcomes and evaluate individual student progress. You can print out copies of these assessments from the accompanying DVD.

Stages of the Unit organize your instruction, guiding your students from inquiry to application.

Focused Instruction provides day-by-day direction for teaching throughout the unit. Each bullet reflects approximately one day of instruction.

Independent Practice links student engagement to Focused Instruction.

Total Days are based on suggested lessons. Numbers of days can be adjusted to meet the needs of your class.

How This Book Will Support You

The Complete Year in Reading and Writing: Kindergarten is written by two authors: Karen McNally, a team leader at LitLife and experienced classroom teacher, and Pam Allyn, the executive director of LitLife. Together, we have spent thousands of hours in kindergarten classrooms, pondering the unique experience that comprises this year.

LitLife is a global organization dedicated to teacher training in the area of literacy education. Every lesson in this book has been field tested in a wide variety of classrooms. LitLife team leaders coach teachers and work alongside students to create a practical, meaningful curriculum that is well suited to each grade level because it exists inside a broader continuum. See this book as a compass you can use to chart a course in reading and writing instruction that feels true to your beliefs about the developmental needs and interests of kindergarteners.

Many programs do not differentiate sufficiently by grade level. Kindergarten grade teachers are often combined into a K–2 grouping in professional literature and workshops. And yet the span between these grades is gigantic—psychologically, socially, and intellectually. A curriculum for kindergarten needs to match the development of the learner and the uniqueness of this age student.

In creating this book for you, we also keep in mind the entirety of the child's learning experience throughout the elementary grades. While specifically written for kindergarteners, the units presented here were created with the big picture in mind, children's entire K–5 experience.

The Complete 4

The Complete 4 was devised in response to the need expressed to us by teachers for balance in literacy instruction. We believe students should be well-rounded readers and writers. This means they should learn about reading and writing strategies. They should also develop a strong understanding of genre and a working knowledge of the conventions of the English language and begin to take on the passions, habits, and behaviors of lifelong readers and writers. The Complete 4 includes four key components of literacy instruction that will help us teach into these varied expectations: Process, Genre, Strategy, and Conventions.

The Complete 4 components help us to plan the school year by balancing the types of units across the year. Knowing whether a unit falls under the category of Process, Genre, Strategy, or Conventions, helps us to focus the unit so that all our lessons lead up to several key understandings.

Here is what we mean by the Complete 4:

Process	Your students will practice the processes shared by all successful readers and writers, at an appropriate developmental level. These include fluency, stamina, and independence.
Genre	Your students will learn to identify and use various literary containers, including narrative, nonfiction, poetry, and standardized tests.
Strategy	Your students will learn to be strategic readers and writers, practicing how writers make plans on a page, and how readers approach text differently depending on their needs.
Conventions	Your students will learn grammar and punctuation in contexts that are real, practical, and relevant to their reading and writing experiences.

In planning a Complete Year of literacy instruction for kindergarten, we have created reading and writing units that reflect a deep balance. All four Complete 4 components are represented. Take a look at the color-coded calendar on the inside front cover of this book to see how these units are organized across the year. We have arranged them so that they build on one another.

Will this book help me connect other aspects of the curriculum to the Complete 4?

Absolutely! One of the best features of the Complete 4 system is its flexibility. It has the capacity to help you integrate all these areas of your curriculum. For example, in kindergarten, your students may be studying various themes such as bears, apples, or pumpkins. They are learning how to make connections across subject areas. Units on nonfiction reading and writing support cross-content work. You can teach the skills and strategies for reading and writing in these thematic areas inside one or more of these units.

Alignment to standards is critical, and these units are constructed in such a way as to reflect the standards and to allow for your adjustments for your state standards.

Can this book help me if I have other demands in my day and cannot teach all the units?

Yes, it can. Here are three suggestions for how you could adapt this calendar to your particular situation:
- You can choose one reading and one writing unit from each Complete 4 component to teach during the year.
- You can focus on the units of study that pair well with your existing themes.
- You can teach only the reading or writing strand.

Will the Complete 4 help me forge reading and writing connections with my students?

This is another great aspect of the Complete 4 program: we link reading and writing units as "companions." Although the instruction may not always be identical, the units should be "talking" to one another. You will see how we take special care to make sure reading and writing units echo and parallel each other, or to stagger them so students see, feel, and understand those essential connections. Indeed, reading and writing are interrelated processes that are mutually supportive when taught together. You may have noticed that your strongest writers are typically your most passionate readers.

Can I use this book to support just my writing instruction since I already use another reading program?

Yes. You can use this book to guide you in either reading or writing. Take a look at the writing calendar only; with your grade-level team, you can look into your reading program and see where you can link the writing units into your instruction. For example, if your reading program has a set of stories on friendship, you could link that set to our Connecting to Story Elements: Reading Fiction unit or our Connecting to Imagination: Writing Fiction unit in the spring. This calendar is designed so that you can use it flexibly: you can use either the reading calendar or the writing calendar on its own or if you want the "complete" package, you can use both of them together. And the Complete 4 is also a way to reintroduce quality children's literature into your classroom even if you use a core reading program.

Can I still benefit from this yearlong approach if my school has commitments that must be addressed at different times of the year?

One of the most exciting aspects of the Complete 4 is that the reading and writing units are interconnected and follow a logical sequence. However, we have also constructed the calendars to allow for flexibility. If, for example, your standardized testing comes earlier in the year, you can easily move units around to suit your test preparation schedule. Or if your entire school studies poetry together in the fall rather than the spring, you can move the units to accommodate that. The calendar is designed to be used either as a whole unit, as a step-by-step program, or as building blocks to construct your own unique program.

Will the Complete 4 help me meet the needs of all learners in my classroom?

The range of ability levels and learning modalities in each of our classrooms reminds us to balance our own teaching. The Complete 4 can help us accomplish this. For example, we tend to work with our English language learners mostly on conventions of print, while we work with writers whose first language is English more on strategies or genre. The Complete 4 reminds us that our English language learners flourish with exposure to the habits and passions of readers and writers, the study of different genres, and practice with complex strategies. Similarly, your students who have a comparatively strong sense of conventions are often not given intensive instruction in that area, but they too would enjoy and benefit greatly from inspiring lessons on the construction of a sentence or the artful use of a punctuation mark. The Complete 4 guides us to teach with an eye to creating a Complete Year for all students.

Will this book help me with the flow of my day?

Yes! We are very aware of your time constraints and the benefits of predictable routines. We have created a very simple, easy-to-follow outline for each day's work during reading and writing time that follows a whole/small/whole pattern. These are the three parts of every lesson:

- Focused Instruction: the whole-class lessons
- Independent Practice: individualized or small-group work
- Wrap-Up: more whole-class teaching with planning for the next day's lesson

Focused Instruction	Students gather for a period of Focused Instruction for 5 to 15 minutes.
	• Warm up your students with a reference to prior teaching and learning.
	• Teach one clear point.
	• Ask students to quickly try your point.
	• Clarify your teaching point.
	• Set the stage for Independent Practice.
Independent Practice	Students practice independently while you confer with students and/or conduct small instructional groups.
	• Encourage students to read or write independently (at their level).
	• Have students practice your teaching point as they read and write.
	• Meet with individual students, partnerships, and/or groups regularly for informal assessment and instruction.
	• Look for future teaching points or an example to use in the Wrap-Up.
Wrap-Up	Students return for a focused, brief discussion that reflects on the day's learning.
	• Restate your teaching point.
	• Share examples of students' work or learning.
	• Set plans for the next day and make connections to homework.

What are my students actually doing during Independent Practice?

As you will see from the scripted lessons in our Spotlight Units, during Independent Practice students practice a skill you have demonstrated. In addition, they are doing something that seems fairly simple on the surface but in fact is the heart of our work and the driving energy for all the lessons in this book: **They are reading**

and writing independently, every day. We suggest that 50 percent of all reading and writing time is Independent Practice. Of this time, approximately 20 percent of their time should be spent practicing a specific skill associated with their reading, and 80 percent of the time should be spent actually reading and writing! Students should be given time every day to read and write in a comfortable manner, at their reading and writing levels and in books and topics that are of great personal interest to them. Here are the approximate amounts of time your students can and should be reading and writing for each day (you may have to work toward these minutes as the year unfolds):

Grade Level	Actual Reading Time	Actual Writing Time
KINDERGARTEN	10–15 minutes	10–20 (writing/drawing)
FIRST GRADE	10–20	10–20
SECOND GRADE	20–30	20–25
THIRD GRADE	30–40	25–30
FOURTH GRADE	35–45	25–30
FIFTH GRADE	40–45	30–40

Are there essential materials I must use in order to make the Complete 4 program a success?

You can use any of your support materials, including a core reading program or a phonics program, alongside the Complete 4 approach. The heart of our approach is that every child has time to practice skills, strategies, and processes through reading and writing that is at his level and is as authentic as possible. A seminal National Endowment for the Arts study (2007) found, not surprisingly, that "students who read for fun nearly every day performed better on reading tests than those who reported reading never or hardly at all." The study points to the "failure of schools and colleges to develop a culture of daily reading habits." In addition, an analysis of federal Department of Education statistics found that those students who scored lower on all standardized tests lived in homes with fewer than ten books. (Rich, 2007). This study then points to two pivotal factors in ensuring lifelong literacy: children must have time to read a lot, and children must have easy, continual access to books.

Our work throughout this book and this series is designed to focus on daily Independent Practice: Students are reading authentic literature and reading a lot, every day, at their own level. Students are writing about topics of authentic interest and writing a lot, every day, at their own level. Students are navigating texts and have easy access to understandable texts throughout the day, especially during literacy time. These then are the two keys to our work: giving students time to practice reading and writing, and giving them access to texts that inspire them both as readers and as writers.

The access is critical and is best accomplished by establishing a well-stocked classroom library. Your library should have a variety of genres: nonfiction, fiction, and poetry. Approximately 20 to 30 percent of your library should be leveled in a clearly organized system in which children can find books that are truly comfortable for them to read at their independent reading levels.

Your students should have a way to bring their books between home and school, and to store the stack of books they have been reading most recently, either in baggies or baskets. Organization is one of two keys to life (the other being passion!). Don't let disorder get in the way of helping your children do a lot of reading in your classroom. They can help you organize your library, too.

It is also crucial for students to have a way to record thinking about reading, either in a reading notebook, or a folder, or even a binder. The important thing to remember is that this should be a system that works for you and your students. It does not matter so much what you select or what you call it, as long as you know your children can easily access it, and they feel comfortable writing in it and, if they are our youngest readers and writers, drawing in it.

During writing time, your students need order as well. Keep a separate writing area neat and stocked, equipped with all the helpful tools a writer loves: sticky notes, staplers, tape, and date stamps. And as with reading time, your students should have a clearly identified, easy-to-use container to capture their writing. In this series we use writing notebooks with our students from second grade to fifth grade, and writing folders with students in kindergarten and first grade. Using folders allows us to provide our students with a variety of paper choices if they need them. The key to keeping containers for students' writing work is that it is easy for them to revisit, reread, and reflect upon, and it is easy for you to look at before conferences and to assess on an ongoing basis. Again, it does not matter what you call these containers, or which ones you choose, as long as they are truly useful for both you and your students.

I don't have access to all the anchor texts you recommend in this book or there are other texts I prefer to use instead. Will my units be as effective if my anchor text selections are somewhat different from yours?

We want to give you as many specific suggestions as we can and so we have recommended many anchor texts for each unit. You can find them both in the Unit Templates and also in the back of the book in a seasonally organized bibliography so you can order all of them for your classroom library if you wish. However, if you can't find them all, or you have others you wish to use instead, you are more than welcome and the units will absolutely be as successful. Take a close look at why we chose the texts we did so you can replace them with selections that will still match the outcomes for the units and will feel comfortable for you.

I use the elements of balanced literacy: shared reading, guided reading, read-aloud, and more. Where do they fit in to the Complete 4 system?

See your elements of balanced literacy as the "how" of your teaching and the Complete 4 as the "what." Teachers who use balanced literacy elements are still asking: But WHAT do I teach tomorrow? The Complete 4 answers that age-old question. Your balanced literacy structures, then, can truly become the engines that drive your content home. For example, shared reading and the read aloud are structures you can use present your content, both in the Focused Instruction and in the Wrap-Up. Guided reading is a structure you can use to practice content with smaller groups of children. This can be done during Independent Practice, so while some of your children are reading independently others are meeting with you in small groups.

What if I've never taught in units like this before?

In a Complete Year unit of study, students learn about one aspect of reading or writing (Process, Genre, Strategy, or Conventions) in a one to six week cycle of learning. Inside this book you will find all the units for a Complete Year of reading and writing instruction. In each unit, we have set a specific focus for instruction and created framing questions to guide you and your students. We have set a time frame and established goals for each unit and put together a list of anchor texts that you can use to teach the lessons. Most important, we have provided helpful templates to take you through *all* the units.

To help you implement and pace your instruction, we have divided the instruction in each unit into four key lesson stages: Immersion, Identification, Guided Practice, and Commitment. The premise behind this concept was inspired by the work of Pearson and Gallagher (1983). They delineated a gradual release of responsibility from teacher to student as the ideal conditions for learning. These stages help us make the necessary turns in our teaching so that we move in an efficient and effective way through any unit of study and our students have the best chance for success.

Immersion	We immerse our students in a topic of study.
Identification	We name or define what students must know about the topic by the end of the unit.
Guided Practice	We model reading and writing for our students and give them time for practice, so that we can guide them toward the goals of the unit.
Commitment	We ask students to reflect on their learning and commit to the use of this knowledge in their future reading and writing.

You use specific language to identify the parts of a unit and the parts of a lesson. How can I be sure I can follow along easily?

The language in this book is extremely user-friendly. We try to steer clear of jargon as much as we can. To best help teachers plan units and teach lessons, we have identified terms that help us all move forward easily. We have included a helpful Glossary of Terms for you on page 233.

What is the role of the Spotlight Units in the Complete Year books?

Each Complete Year book features eight bonus Spotlight Units, designed to help you understand what each unit of study can look and feel like in your classroom—both in terms of the concrete day-to-day details as well as the "learning energy" that you create through your instructional language and strategies. During the Spotlight Units, we invite you into our classrooms to sit by our sides and listen as we interact with our students. While we know you'll use your own language that reflects your unique teaching personality, we provide examples of language we use in our classrooms as a model for you to adapt. Learning how to craft our teaching language in artful ways that encourage active student participation takes practice; for example, knowing how to design open-ended questions rather than questions that just elicit a yes–no response is an art, typically learned through classroom-tested trial and error. Sometimes it's helpful to listen in on another teacher and notice how she uses language to frame each teaching moment.

Inside the Spotlight Units, you'll find one reading unit and one writing unit in each of the Complete 4 components (Process, Genre, Strategy, and Conventions). Our Spotlight Units also include unit templates, so you can see how we translate the templates into day-by-day lesson plans. You'll notice that not all bullets are translated directly into lessons and that the flow of the unit is fluid and flexible so you can adapt it in ways that fit your students' unique needs and interests.

How do I use the unit templates?

We envision teachers taking the templates we provide for each unit and adapting them to their students. Perhaps you have favorite books you love to read in your nonfiction unit. Or perhaps your students need more than one day on a bulleted lesson. Although the templates offer guidelines for the overall structure of a unit and suggestions for how the unit might be paced, we see them as a road atlas, a guide that leads you toward your goal but also gives you the opportunity to add your own special touches along the way. Many teachers like to keep these unit templates on their desks as a reminder of where they are going, to help them plan each day's lesson.

How will I assess my students through the Complete Year?

The structure of the Complete 4 classroom gives you a rich opportunity to assess your students during their Independent Practice. Units of study give you regular, frequent opportunities to take stock of your students' progress. At the end of each unit is an assessment form for you to use.

Chapter 6 is dedicated to the C4 Assessment (C4A): a comprehensive tool designed for your grade level. You can use the C4A three times a year for both reading and writing. Quick and easy, the C4A will provide valuable information on your students' progress in all areas of reading and writing instruction.

The Complete Year in Kindergarten

Our learning time with our students, bound by the parameters of the school year, is organized by seasons. We thought it would be helpful to organize our books that way, too.

For kindergarteners the profundity of the first season is in its newness—the raw energy of entering into a new place for the first time. By late fall and early winter, your kindergarteners are adjusting to school, feeling like "big" kids, clasping their lunch boxes proudly, knowing the way to the principal's office, finally. In winter they are deep into their learning, digging into the alphabet and numbers, experts in their classroom routines, but still longing for home and a nap on more than one occasion. With spring comes a different kind of energy: while some of your children are really reading and writing by now, there are signs of struggle in others; you are worrying about them. Social structures shift continuously; they make new friends and circle around one another, learning, investigating: Who am I becoming? Late spring is a time of wonder and joy: We made it! There is a celebration in the air: soon to become first graders, the students ponder their newfound independence, but still want to hold their teacher's hand on the way to lunch.

Get ready now for the Complete Year experience. It's timely and timeless (and won't cost YOU time). Flexible and friendly (and fun). Easy to use and easy to navigate (and easy to explain to parents). Standards-based and field-tested (in hundreds of classrooms). Made for you (to simplify your teaching life and to reconnect you with the joy of teaching). Made for your kindergarteners (especially).

Have a great year!

Chapter 2

EARLY FALL

The Kindergartener as Story Creator

"In the universe, on a planet, on a continent, in a country, in a city, on a block, in a house, in a window, in the rain, a little girl named Madlenka finds out her tooth wiggles. She has to tell everyone."

—from *Madlenka* by Peter Sis

Your kindergarteners are full to the brim of the joy of being in a new learning community. They are also at the same time aware of their smallness in a big world. This season is about creating safe, predictable structures for the reading and writing experiences that will shape their sense of themselves for the rest of their lives. Like Madlenka, the kindergartener opens her arms to experience, to people, to the sense of her own newfound power expressed through explorations of play and literacy. Join us as we greet the new school year with units of study especially designed for kindergarteners during the first season of the year.

EARLY FALL UNITS

SPOTLIGHT UNITS

Beginning the Year With the ARCH

Our first units, known as the ARCH, are designed to bring our students together into a reading and writing community. This acronym stands for Assessment, Routines, Choice, and Healthy Community. The units balance the need to assess students as readers and writers with lessons on the routines of reading and writing time, the community-building aspects of reading and writing time, and how to make choices both in terms of topics and texts.

We must actively construct this community, by establishing the daily routines for reading and writing time, discovering personal and shared interests, and introducing our students to our libraries and writing tools. Fountas and Pinnell (2001) remind us that during the first month of school you have two important goals: to help your students think of themselves as readers and to establish roles and routines. They remind us to repeat key lessons, chart the routines and roles of the reader and writer, and refer our students back to these reference points regularly.

As teachers, we are always a bit uncertain about how to begin the year in terms of content. We want to get to know our students, and we know we need to establish these routines, but we wonder what the content and outcomes are for this work. The ARCH is designed to blend both process and products: the beautiful work we do in coming together for the first time, as well as the important work we do in generating products that represent our students and move them forward at the very beginning of this school year's journey.

Each Complete 4 year begins with an ARCH unit at every grade level, but each year should feel different because of your students' changing developmental needs. (See page 112 of *The Complete 4 for Literacy* to see all the ARCH articulations for each grade level.) In kindergarten, our ARCH focus is Home/School Connections. In the reading and writing units that follow, we continue to build upon that theme with units that help our students discover their preferences and set goals as readers and writers.

The ARCH units set the foundation for the entire year. The ARCH incorporates teaching of all of those routines and habits you long for and need when you are in the midst of your work with your students. If you set the stage now, you are guaranteed a happy, truly productive year in the teaching of reading and writing.

The ARCH: Home/School Connections in Reading

Why Teach This?
- To help students recognize routines of reading time.
- To determine students' strengths and needs as the year begins.
- To create a supportive reading community with students.
- To help students forge home/school connections in literacy.

Framing Questions
- How are we developing a sense of ourselves as readers?
- How are we building a reading community?
- What are the books we want to read that match us as readers?

Unit Goals
- Students will understand and follow the routines of reading time.
- Students will make book choices that match their interests and purposes.
- Students will share books and their thinking about books with a partner.

Anchor Texts
- *A Bedtime Story* by Mem Fox
- *A Box Full of Kittens* by Sonia Manzano
- *My Kindergarten* by Rosemary Wells
- *The Napping House* by Audrey Wood
- *Please, Puppy, Please* by Spike Lee and Tanya Lewis Lee
- *Reading Makes You Feel Good* by Todd Parr
- *Rescue Vehicles* (*Big Stuff* series) by Robert Gould

Unit Assessment The ARCH: Home/School Connections in Reading			PROCESS
Student name:	EMERGING	DEVELOPING	INDEPENDENT
Follows routines of reading time with assistance.			
Makes book selections with assistance.			
Identifies reading interests.			
Identifies reasons why people read.			
Works with a partner to share a book with assistance.			

Stage of the Unit	Focused Instruction You will	Independent Practice Students will
IMMERSION 5 days	• reflect on your reading habits and preferences; use *Rescue Vehicles* and *Please, Puppy, Please* to demonstrate to readers choices in books (differences in genres).	• explore their own preferences and habits by touring the library and talking to other readers.

IMMERSION *(continued)*	• share a special reading memory; read *A Bedtime Story*. • read a selection from *My Kindergarten* and share your own goals for the reading year. • share thoughts on what it means to be a member of a reading community (sharing book suggestions, talking about books, having quiet time for reading). • invite guest readers in to read and to talk about how reading is important to them.	• draw a picture of a special reading memory. • build a working definition of what it means to be part of a reading community (listening, sharing, enjoying). • browse books independently or with informal partners. • draw pictures of themselves as readers.
IDENTIFICATION 3 days	• identify what readers do during reading time. • model selecting books for interest and comfort level. • make (with students) a list of why people read; read *Reading Makes You Feel Good*.	• identify behaviors that represent participation in a reading community (one-inch voices, listening to others, sharing ideas). • browse and read independently or with a partner.
GUIDED PRACTICE 4 days	• model the kinds of things readers do during reading time (browse, linger with the pictures, use one-inch voices to talk about books). • use *A Box Full of Kittens* to demonstrate what readers do when they are finished with a book (reread, find a favorite part, share with a partner, choose a new book from the basket). • read *The Napping House* and model aloud what readers think about when they read. • model how readers share their ideas about books with each other (book is placed between both students, pointing to specifics on a page, listening to one another).	• practice thinking habits while they look at pictures in books or read the print, if they can (stop to question, stop to reflect). • read independently or with a partner with a new awareness of what to do when finished with a book. • practice sharing their book ideas with others.
COMMITMENT 1 day	• model goal setting for the year (as readers, we will. . .).	• choose a favorite book from this unit to share with a friend. • discuss what they now can do as readers. • discuss what they would like to be able to do as readers by the end of the year.
TOTAL: 13 DAYS		

The ARCH: Home/School Connections in Writing

Why Teach This?

- To help students recognize routines of writing time.
- To determine students' strengths and needs as the year begins.
- To have students participate in a supportive writing community.
- To help students forge home/school connections in literacy.

Framing Questions

- How are we developing a sense of ourselves as writers?
- How are we building a writing community?
- What are the tools we use as writers?

Unit Goals

- Students will understand and follow the routines of writing time.
- Students will generate writing ideas.
- Students will understand how to use writing materials and resources.
- Students will represent their ideas through drawings and/or words.

Anchor Texts

- *A Box Full of Kittens* by Sonia Manzano
- *Goodnight, Moon* by Margaret Wise Brown
- *I Want to Be* by Thylias Moss
- *Koala Lou* by Mem Fox
- *My Kindergarten* by Rosemary Wells
- *The Napping House* by Audrey Wood

Resource Sheets

- Alphabet Chart (Resource 2.1)
- Personalized Writing Folders (Resource 2.2)
- Paper Samples for Early Fall Units (Resources 2.8–2.11)

Unit Assessment The ARCH: Home/School Connections in Writing			PROCESS
Student name:	EMERGING	DEVELOPING	INDEPENDENT
Follows routines of writing time with assistance.			
Generates writing ideas with assistance.			
Uses alphabet chart with assistance.			
Identifies reasons why people write.			
Works with a partner to tell a story with assistance.			

Stage of the Unit	Focused Instruction You will	Independent Practice Students will
IMMERSION 3 days	• reflect on your writing preferences and habits (where, when, and what you like to write). • demonstrate how you personalize your writing folder (see Resource 2.2, Personalizing Writing Folders). • have students generate a baseline piece of writing (picture drawing) to be used for assessment.	• explore their own writing preferences by thinking, writing, and talking to other writers. • draw a picture of where they like to write. • personalize their writing folders with photos and words that represent them. • write or draw ideas of their own.
IDENTIFICATION 3 days	• show purposes for the writing folder (for finished pieces and for drafts). • create a list of the kinds of writing people do. • model the Four Prompts (I wonder, I remember, I observe, I imagine).	• generate a list of possible writing topics by drawing them and sharing with a partner. • discuss with a partner the kinds of things they would like to create as writers (letters, lists, poems). • write or draw ideas generated from the Four Prompts.
GUIDED PRACTICE 7 days	• model how to use a writing folder and how to select paper, model use of different kinds of paper. • read *A Box Full of Kittens* and demonstrate "writing": drawing, sketching, telling stories, putting print on the page. • demonstrate that writers write about what feels important — what they wonder about, remember, observe, and imagine (the Four Prompts). • model use of an alphabet chart. • model a conference and explain the procedures. • study an anchor text with students such as *Goodnight Moon* by Margaret Wise Brown or *Koala Lou* by Mem Fox: Where did the writing idea come from? Create a writing ideas chart. • model how children respond to one another during a Wrap-Up.	• select different kinds of paper to match the writing purpose and level of the writer: paper without lines, paper with one line, paper with picture boxes. (See Resources 2.8–2.11) • convey ideas through pictures and/or words. • practice writing to one of the Four Prompts. • practice using an alphabet chart. • browse through picture books to add to writing ideas chart. • practice sharing their writing with a partner.

COMMITMENT 1 day	• admire participation in writing community and name those qualities. • celebrate your first piece of writing.	• draw themselves as writers. • share one piece they have created in a celebration.
TOTAL: 14 DAYS		

SPOTLIGHT on Process

- Reading Stories Through Pictures
- Telling Stories Through Pictures and Words

In my book *The Complete 4 for Literacy*, I explain in detail how process units are designed to build identity, capacity, collaboration, and responsibility. Although these form the foundation upon which readers and writers grow, they are so intangible that they often take a back seat in our instructional plans. A student's understanding of herself and the actions that move her forward as a reader and writer are an important part of her growth as a kindergartener. Establishing a strong understanding of processes now will help us move forward smoothly, rather than having to grapple with management issues later on in the year. Our explicit instructions for working with a partner give our students a structure for growing ideas and supporting one another. Lessons on building community will create a spirit of joy and collaboration that is indispensable in sustaining the atmosphere of safety and trust in your room. In these units students learn how to use books to tell stories, how to explore stories, and how to tell their own stories in powerful ways. For more information on process units, please see pages 37–47 of my book *The Complete 4 for Literacy*.

Pam Allyn

Story Matters

In *Grand Conversations: Literature Groups in Action*, Ralph Peterson and Maryann Eeds (2007) describe story as "an exploration and illumination of life."

The two units featured in this chapter are predicated on the idea that story drives us as human beings and that children have powerful reasons to tell stories that propel them toward literacy. You will see that the preeminence of story as a foundational idea that stretches across all kindergarteners do is a major theme throughout this book. The researcher Elizabeth Sulzby (1991) notes that children's literacy development is sustained and nurtured through their social interactions with caring adults and exposure to storybooks.

Reading Stories Through Pictures

PROCESS

Why Teach This?

- To help students develop an understanding of story structure.
- To enable students to identify book language as different from conversational language.
- To help students understand that a story is told through pictures and words.

Framing Questions

- How can we read a story if we cannot read the words?
- What do all stories have in common?
- How can we use what we know about letters and words to read the words in our books?

Unit Goals

- Students will use picture walks to activate prior knowledge and set a context for telling or reading the story.
- Students will recognize story elements in the stories they are reading.
- Students will understand that pictures combined with words tell a story.

Anchor Texts

- *The Gingerbread Man* by Catherine McCafferty
- *Goldilocks and the Three Bears* by Byron Barton
- *How Rabbit Tricked Otter* by Gayle Ross
- *Jack and the Beanstalk* by Carol Ottelenghi
- *Kiss Good Night* by Amy Hest
- *The Kissing Hand* by Audrey Penn
- *Mama Panya's Pancakes: A Village Tale From Kenya* by Mary Chamberlin
- *The Three Billy Goats Gruff* by Stephen Carpenter
- *The Three Little Pigs* by Patricia Siebert
- *Where the Wild Things Are* by Maurice Sendak
- *Yeh-Shen: A Cinderella Story from China* by Ai-Ling Louie

Resource Sheets

- Alphabet Chart (Resource 2.1)
- Parent Letter (Resource 2.3)

Unit Assessment Reading Stories Through Pictures			PROCESS
Student name:	EMERGING	DEVELOPING	INDEPENDENT
Uses picture walks to enhance meaning.			
Recognizes story elements.			
Connects pictures to words on the page.			
Uses story language while reading.			
Uses transitional words to string pictures in the book together.			

Stage of the Unit	Focused Instruction You will	Independent Practice Students will
IMMERSION 4 days	• read aloud from *The Gingerbread Man* and demonstrate taking a picture walk through the book. • using *The Three Little Pigs*, demonstrate how to read a story by looking at pictures in a book and remembering the story on each page. • notice familiar letters and words in books.	• explore familiar books by taking picture walks. • read stories using pictures and prior knowledge of a book. • explore the print in books to locate familiar letters or words.
IDENTIFICATION 1 day	• read aloud from *Jack and the Beanstalk* and name the story elements (character, setting, problem/solution). • give the analogy of ingredients in a cake to ingredients in a story.	• identify and name story elements in a familiar book.
GUIDED PRACTICE 10 days	• read aloud from *The Kissing Hand* and demonstrate how to identify story elements in the stories we read. • model identifying and using character names when reading pictures (use *The Three Little Pigs*, *The Gingerbread Man*, and *Jack and the Beanstalk*). • demonstrate bringing characters to life by using different character voices. • model identifying setting and including a statement of time and/or place when reading the pictures. • read aloud from *Goldilocks and the Three Bears* and model the use of transitional words to sequence events in a story.	• read stories guided by their knowledge of story elements in each particular story. • remember and include character names when reading a story. • use different voices to represent different characters. • remember and include a reference to time and/or place when reading a story. • practice using transitional words to link plot events together. • begin to use story language when telling stories. • tell stories using stringing words.

GUIDED PRACTICE (continued)	• read aloud from *Little Red Riding Hood* and model how to distinguish between story language and conversational language. • read aloud from *Where the Wild Things Are* and identify stringing words in a story. • find familiar letters and words in the print of a book using word rings. • read aloud from *The Three Little Pigs*, *Where the Wild Things Are*, and *The Three Billy Goats Gruff* to model how words and phrases are repeated in some books. • demonstrate looking for specific words you expect to find on a particular page. • use *Where the Wild Things Are* to help students take a picture walk then tell the story.	• look for familiar letters and words in the print of their book. • look for specific words they know to be written on a particular page.
COMMITMENT 1 day	• guide students through a reflection process: "What I now know about stories; what I can now do as a reader." • transcribe students' reflective statements to serve as an assessment and celebration piece.	• orally reflect on their knowledge of story and on their growth as readers.
TOTAL: 16 DAYS		

Getting Started

In this unit, you will teach your students how to apply story structure and language to their own stories after spending time identifying and integrating these elements in reading time.

Structures and Routines

Partnerships

Students practice what was taught in the whole-class lesson independently. Then students meet with reading partners to tell their stories to one another.

We suggest that you create partners for this unit based on:

- similar book interests (for example, both students like to read fairy tales)
- compatibility (students who feel comfortable and productive working together)
- verbal skills (either a heterogeneous or homogeneous match will work)
- understanding of print (pairing those students together who are similar in their understanding of print concepts)

Teaching Materials

Setting up Book Baskets

Fairy Tales and Folktales

You will find both classic and alternative versions to popular fairy tales and folktales.

Paul Galdone is a prolific author who has written versions of many titles, including *The Three Little Pigs, The Gingerbread Boy, The Three Billy Goats Gruff,* and *The Three Bears*. Many of these titles are available in big book size. Below is a list of other classic versions of the most popular titles along with a corresponding alternative version of the same story.

Classic Tale	Author	Alternative Tale	Author
Jack and the Beanstalk	Carol Ottelenghi	*Jack and the Beanstalk/Giants Have Feelings, Too (Another Point of View)*	Alvin Grawowsky
The Three Little Pigs	Patricia Seibert	*The Three Little Wolves and the Big Bad Pig*	Eugene Trivizas
The Gingerbread Man	Catherine McCafferty	*The Gingerbread Girl*	Lisa Campbell Ernst
The Three Bears ("Goldilocks")	Byron Barton	*Goldilocks Returns* *The Three Snow Bears*	Lisa Campbell Ernst Jan Brett
The Three Billy Goats Gruff	Stephen Carpenter	*The Three Billy Goats Gruff/Just a Friendly Old Troll (Another Point of View)*	Alvin Granowsky

For our most emergent readers, take a look at the Easy to Read Folktales series as well as the Rigby PM Collection Orange, Tales and Plays, published by Rigby Books.

Picture Books

In addition to the anchor texts, these picture books work well for this unit because they have strong picture support and a clear narrative arc.

- *Anansi the Spider: A Tale from the Ashanti* by Gerald McDermott
- *Bear Feels Sick* by Karma Wilson
- *Beautiful Blackbirds* by Ashley Bryan
- *A Chair for Baby Bear* by Kaye Umansky
- *A Good Day* by Kevin Henkes
- *How to Catch a Star* by Oliver Jeffers
- *Kitten's First Full Moon* by Kevin Henkes
- *Leaves* by David Ezra Stein
- *Leo the Late Bloomer* by Robert Kraus
- *Library Lion* by Michelle Knudson
- *Lost and Found* by Oliver Jeffers
- *The Mitten* by Jan Brett

- Moon Bear books by Frank Asch, especially *Happy Birthday Moon*
- *Owen* by Kevin Henkes
- *The Paper Princess* by Elisa Kleven
- *Tacky the Penguin* by Helen Lester and Lynn M. Munsinger
- *Why Mosquitoes Buzz in People's Ears* by Verna Aardema

Differentiation

Some of your students are already reading at this early point in the year. We want these students lingering with the pictures in their books like their classmates, but we want to give them every opportunity to practice decoding print. Below we have listed two series for beginning readers that support the picture work you will be teaching in the unit and also tell the story through words.

- The Brand New Readers Series by Candlewick Press
- Elephant and Piggie series by Mo Willems

Student Materials

Alphabet Chart (see Resource 2.1)

Students can use this alphabet chart to locate or identify particular letters as they read.

Sticky Notes

Students will mark familiar sight words with a sticky note in their books. We like to use the very small arrow-shaped notes.

Word Rings

Metal rings hold index cards with familiar sight words written on them. As they read, students use their rings to search for these words in their books. For writing, they serve as a spelling resource.

A student uses a word ring to find a word in her book.

Stages of the Unit

Immersion

Students learn how to take a picture walk in a book to get a sense of what the story is about. Demonstrate how the pictures in a book can tell a story when the text is too complex to read independently. A parent letter can be sent home at this time (see Resource 2.3).

Identification

The Identification lesson lists the story elements that are included in the stories students tell (and read). These should include character, setting, and plot events. While we may not use the literary term "plot events" with our five-year-olds, we do explain that there are important things

Story Ingredients

Characters

Setting

Important events in the story

- problem
- solution

Story language

that happen in a story, and we include those in our story; often there is a problem in the story, and we want to make sure to tell about that part.

Guided Practice

Demonstrate for students:

- how to tell a story that includes key story elements
- how to use linking words to string together pictures into a story and
- how to incorporate story language such as "once upon a time" into their stories.

The progression of stories that kindergarteners tell goes from fairy tales and folktales to familiar picture books (read-alouds they have heard before) to new books. This progression builds student confidence and understanding of story elements with familiar stories, which is then applied to unfamiliar wordless books.

fairy tales and folktales ⟶ familiar picture books ⟶ new picture books

Commitment

At the end of the unit, students reflect on what they have learned about reading stories. Record their oral reflection statements as a form of assessment.

How to Use the Lessons in the Spotlight Units

In every Spotlight Unit, we have scripted out each lesson: the Focused Instruction, the Independent Practice, and the Wrap-Up. Where you see italics, we have provided model language: you are free to use it as is, or you may prefer to adapt the language to suit your needs. For example, if we mention a book we might read aloud to our class, and you have one you like better, feel free to use that one instead. Or if we use a personal anecdote as a demonstration, you should replace it with one of your own. Where there are no italics, the lesson plan includes guidelines for what you and the students could be doing at that point in the lesson. You will notice that there is always a balance of teacher talk and suggested actions.

Day-by-Day Lessons

DAY 1 Immersion

Focused Instruction

We are starting a new unit of study today that will teach you how to read stories using pictures to help you. I am going to use this big book version of The Gingerbread Man *to show you how readers take what is called a picture walk. Notice how I turn the pages and talk about what I see in each picture.*

- Model taking a picture walk. The emphasis is on your observations without naming specifics about setting, character names, or specific plot points.
- Lead students through a picture walk on the next two or three pages of the big book.

Independent Practice

There are baskets of books on your tables with fairy tales and folktales. Work with your reading partner to choose a book and take a picture walk, just like we practiced together.

- Students choose a book from a tabletop basket and take a picture walk with their partners.

Wrap-Up

- Students share experiences taking picture walks with a partner.

DAY 2 Immersion

Focused Instruction

Today I am going to show you how to take a picture walk and then go back and tell a story to go with the pictures. Listen to how I name what I notice in the pictures.

- Take a picture walk through the beginning of *The Three Little Pigs*, focusing on your observations from the illustrations.

Now I am going to tell a story to go with the pictures. Listen to how this sounds different from my picture walk.

- Tell a story from those same pictures, but this time incorporate story language like "once upon a time," character names, character voices, transitional words, and a story. It should sound like you are reading a story, not just making observations about the pictures.

How did this sound different than my picture walk? What did you notice?

- Students are asked to think about how this storytelling sounds different from a picture walk.

Independent Practice

Work with your partner to choose a book from your tabletop basket. Take a picture walk through your book first, and then go back and tell the story by looking at the pictures. Remember that the story you tell should sound different from your picture walk. It is not just describing what you see in the pictures, it is telling the story you saw when you looked at all the pictures together.

- Differentiating Instruction
  - Strong readers take a picture walk and then go back to read the words. These students work independently, then meet with their partner and take turns reading their books to each other and sharing stories with each other using story language.

Wrap-Up

When you are not able to read the words in a book, you can look at the pictures and let them remind you of how the story goes; you can tell the story by looking at the pictures.

- Ask two partnerships to share the beginning of a story they told.

DAY 3 Immersion

Focused Instruction

I will do a picture walk through The Three Little Pigs, *and then I will go back and "read" it as a story, using story language. Listen for how I make my story sound like a story.*

- Model doing a picture walk with *Goldilocks*, then "read" the story you saw through the pictures. Emphasize the use of transitional words and story language (e.g., "once upon a time").

Independent Practice

You will be working with your reading partner to take a picture walk in a book and then tell the story that goes with the pictures.

- Partners work together to choose a book from their tabletop basket, take a picture walk, and then tell the story to go with the pictures.

Wrap-Up

- Use a big book version of a fairy tale or another favorite story and tell it through the pictures as a class.

DAY 4 Immersion

Focused Instruction

You have been using the pictures in fairy tales and folktales to tell stories with your reading partner. Pictures, together with the words on the page, are what tell the story— they help each other. Up to this point we have only been looking at pictures. Today we will turn our attention to the words on the page. Yesterday I told the story of The Three Little Pigs *through the pictures. Watch me as I turn to the first page, briefly look at the picture, and then look at the words on the bottom of the page.*

- Demonstrate looking for a single letter—the letter "P" for "Pig."
- Demonstrate looking for a familiar word on the page.
- Demonstrate figuring out a word you do not know well.

Did you notice how I looked carefully to see if there were any words I could figure out? I did not get frustrated if I didn't know some of them, but I really tried with each one.

Independent Practice

You will find new books in your tabletop baskets today. First use the pictures to learn more about the book and do either a picture walk or tell the story using the pictures. Then I would like you to take some time with the words in your book. You can try some of the things I did to figure them out: look at the first letter, look for words you know, try to figure out the word just like I did.

- After 10 minutes of focusing on pictures, students look at the words in their book.

Wrap-Up

- Choose two partnerships to share their reading experiences.

DAY 5 Identification

Focused Instruction

You have spent the last few days taking picture walks and telling stories by looking at the pictures in books. Telling a story is like baking a cake. When you bake, there are certain ingredients—such as flour, sugar, and butter—that you must mix together in order to come out with a cake. When we tell a story, there are certain ingredients—called story ingredients—that you must mix together to make a story. As we read Jack and the Beanstalk, *let's think about some of those story ingredients. Let's try to name them together.*

- Chart student responses. Their responses from Day 3 can be revisited to get the conversation started if necessary. The chart should contain the basic story elements: character, setting, and important events.

When you are telling a story to go with the pictures in your book today, mix in our story ingredients when you tell it.

Independent Practice

- Partnerships take picture walks and tell stories to go with pictures in their books with a new awareness of story ingredients.

Wrap-Up

- Recount what partnerships did in their work today. Identify two students who really integrated story ingredients in their storytelling. Have those students share the ingredients they found.

DAY 6 Guided Practice

Focused Instruction

I am going to tell the story of The Kissing Hand *by Audrey Penn by looking at the pictures. When you hear me mix in one of the story ingredients, give me a thumbs-up.*

- Model telling the story through pictures, including transitional words and character voices. Integrate the story elements into the story you tell.

Independent Practice

Look at our story ingredients chart. With your partner, find each ingredient in your story. Then go back and tell the story

Wrap-Up

- Student partners share work. Identify two partnerships that correctly identified all the story ingredients. Have these partnerships share with the class.

DAY 7 Guided Practice

Focused Instruction

One ingredient we mix into our stories is information about the characters in the book. A character can be a person or an animal. When we tell our stories we want to include the names of characters. I am going to show you some pictures of characters in different stories we know. Let's see how many of them we can name.

Independent Practice

When you are telling your stories today, remember to include character names.

- Students look for character names.
- Strong readers are asked to find the names of their characters in the print.

Wrap-Up

- Show several books the students know and in a fun, game-like way see if they can remember the names of the characters.

DAY 8 Guided Practice

Focused Instruction

Today we are going to think about how your characters may sound when they are talking, and we'll use their voices when we are telling the story. I am going to read to you Kiss Good Night. *The characters are Mrs. Bear and Sam. Listen to me as I imagine how each character would sound and then tell the story that way. Did you hear how I made my voice sound like a child and then like a mom? Let's practice telling more of the story together.*

- Show the next pages of the story.
- Students practice telling that part of the story to a partner using character voices.

Independent Practice

Talk with your partner about the characters in your book and how they might sound. When you are telling (or reading) the story, make your voice sound the way you imagine the characters would sound in real life.

Wrap-Up

- Two students tell a portion of their stories to the class sharing the character voices they created from their stories.

DAY 9 Guided Practice

Focused Instruction

You have spent the past few days using the pictures to think about the characters in your books. We know that the pictures are just part of what tells a story. The words on a page also tell the story. Today you are going to revisit a book you have read before and look at the words that accompany the pictures. I am going to use my alphabet chart to find the letter that starts the character's name.

- Use the pictures on an alphabet chart to locate the letter "S."

Now I am going to look for the letter "S" on this page and see if it is in Sam's name. Today, use your alphabet charts and partner's help to find characters' names in your books and read them.

Independent Practice

You and your partner will revisit a book you have read before. See if you can find the name on the page. (Stronger readers can do this quickly and then read the text.)

Wrap-Up

- Demonstrate finding character names in *Goldilocks and the Three Bears.*

DAY 10 Guided Practice

Focused Instruction

Setting is one of our story ingredients—it is where the story is happening. Where does the story Mama Panya's Pancakes: A Village Tale From Kenya *take place? In the first half of the book, the setting is outdoors. Let us look at how the author and illustrator Jerry Pinkney describes setting in the first half of the book. In the second half of the book, the setting changes to the grandma's house. Let us look at the pictures together. Turn to your partner and talk about how the illustrator conveys the mood of the story through the setting.*

Independent Practice

Work with your partner and talk about what the setting is in your story. When you go back and tell the story, be sure to include the setting.

Wrap-Up

I want us to go around the classroom and say the one or two words that describe the setting of the story you told today.

DAY 11 Guided Practice

Focused Instruction

When we tell stories, there are words we use to connect the things that happened. For example, listen to me tell the story about our fire drill yesterday. "We were all in math centers yesterday morning, **then** *we heard the fire alarm.* **First**, *we lined up quietly at the door.* **After that**, *we walked through the hall and outside to our special meeting area.* **Finally**, *when we learned everything was safe, we went back inside." I use words like* "then," "after that," and "finally" to string together the things that happened in my story. When we tell stories in our books, we need to string together the things that happen in the same way. Listen to me as I string together the things that happen in Where the Wild Things Are with special words I'll call "stringing words." "Max was sent to his room without dinner because he caused mischief. That night a forest grew in his bedroom. **Then** he saw a boat and sailed away in it. He sailed in the boat for a long time and **finally** reached an island. **After that,** he met the wild things." Who heard some stringing words I used to tell this story?

- Use a thick piece of string, write the stringing words on index cards and attach to the string.
- Remember to use some code or visual cue that will remind the students of what the word says.

Independent Practice

Today when you are telling the stories in your books, use stringing words to tell about things happening one after another. If you use a stringing word we haven't discussed yet, try to remember it and we will add it to our list of words.

- Differentiating Instruction
  - Strong readers can look for stringing words in their book and write them on a sticky note.

Wrap-Up

- Ask students to give you a thumbs-up if they were able to use stringing words when telling their stories. Add any additional words to your list.

DAY 12 Guided Practice

Focused Instruction

We know that words and pictures tell a story. Over the past few days you have been learning to read in our big books and the messages I write to the class. Everyone has their own ring with our word-wall words on them. After telling your story through the pictures, you will go back and look for our word-wall words in your books. Watch me as I do this work in one of our big book stories.

Independent Practice

I have your word rings out at your reading spots. Remember to look for those words when you are done telling the story through the pictures. I am giving each partnership two sticky notes. If you find one of those words in your story, mark it with a note.

- Differentiating Instruction
  - Vulnerable readers continue to hunt for specific letters rather than words.
  - Strong readers continue to read the complete text.

Wrap-Up

- Students who have found word-ring words in their books read them to the class.

DAY 13 Guided Practice

Focused Instruction

Today we are going to think about the sound of stories—the words that are used in stories that are different from words we use when we are talking to one another. The Three Billy Goats Gruff *begins, "Once upon a time there were three billy goats gruff." We do not talk to one another like that. I would not say to you, "Once upon a time I was on vacation at the beach!" Here is another book we know,* Kiss Good Night. *The first page says, "It was a dark and stormy night on Plum Street." The beginnings of* Three Billy Goats Gruff *and* Kiss Good Night *have great story language. When you hear those words you know they come right out of a book. When you are telling the stories today, use this story language to begin them.*

Independent Practice

In your books today, try beginning with story language—words that sound like a book.

- Differentiating Instruction

Strong readers: Pay attention to the way your stories begin. Does your book have great story language? If so, mark it with a sticky note and share with the class during the Wrap-Up.

Wrap-Up

As I was conferring with you, I wrote down some of the story language I heard you use in your books. Listen to this...

DAY 14 Guided Practice

Focused Instruction

We have been studying the sound of stories—words and phrases that you would only find in a book and wouldn't use when you are talking to a friend. Today I want you to notice how stories will often repeat words or phrases. Listen to the repeated line in The Three Little Pigs: *"And he huffed and he puffed and he blew the house down." In* Where the Wild Things Are *the forest in Max's room "grew and grew and grew..." In* The Three Billy Goats Gruff, *"Trip, trap, trip, trap." When you are telling your stories today, try to use repeating words or phrases like we heard in these books.*

Independent Practice

- Students incorporate repeating story language into the stories they are telling. Early readers are looking for places in their books that have repeating story language and marking them with a sticky note.

Wrap-Up

- Share repeating story language you heard students using in their books.

DAY 15 Guided Practice

Focused Instruction

Today we will read Where the Wild Things Are. *We are going to work together as a class to tell the story. We will go around the circle, and everyone will get a chance to tell a part of the story. Remember all we have learned about story ingredients and the sound of stories. Let's take a picture walk first. Then we can tell a great story just through the pictures.*

- Highlight story elements, transitional words, and examples of story language as students use them to tell the story.

Independent Practice

When you are telling your stories today, try to use all that you have learned about story ingredients, stringing words, and story language.

- Students incorporate all they have learned when telling (or reading) stories from their baskets.

Wrap-Up

- Choose a pair of students to share a portion of the story they told in Independent Practice. Their story should exemplify some aspect of the instruction in this unit you want others to incorporate into their work.

DAY 16 Commitment

Focused Instruction

Today you are going to reflect on what you have learned about stories. "To reflect" means to look back on yourself—like looking at your reflection in a mirror. Reflecting on something you have learned feels good and reminds you of what you can now do that you couldn't do before. What have you learned about telling (and reading) stories that you did not know before this unit? What can you do now in your books that you could not do before?

- Record students' oral reflections. You may want to display student comments in a public place for all to appreciate.

Independent Practice

- Display all the books you used in the unit. Have a "story party." Students meet with friends, choose a favorite book, and use the pictures to tell the story— together or by taking turns.

Wrap-Up

- We will be starting a new unit tomorrow but don't worry, these books won't go away! I will keep them in our library area for you to read at play time and rest time. We will also be using some of these books later in the year for other units.

Magical Storytelling

Varied storytelling is useful for different reasons. First the kindergartener wants to be "big" more than anything: she is expansive, generous, and open in the way she lives and the way she tells stories. The expansiveness that accompanies her retelling of stories is all part of her growth experience: it builds stamina and, on the page, it builds fluency. To deny a kindergartener the opportunity to tell an expansive story on the page or orally is to be inattentive to her developmental needs.

Kindergarteners really do believe in magic! They are moving back and forth constantly between an imaginary universe and what is real around them. This unit seek to bridge those worlds and help our children understand that there is power in what they know and what they imagine as possible writing topics. Some students feel more comfortable telling imaginary stories while others prefer to tell you about their visit to their grandmother's house. A unit in storytelling honors both entry points. This unit is not about fantasy versus reality, but rather about the nature of story itself, which encompasses both of those worlds. Kindergarteners know better than anyone how to make the ordinary extraordinary, and that is what storytelling is all about.

Telling Stories Through Pictures and Words

PROCESS

Why Teach This?
- To teach students to tell sequential stories.
- To teach students how to find story ideas.
- To develop students' listening skills.
- To deepen students' understanding of story structure and story language.

Framing Questions
- How do we tell a story that makes sense and is in order?
- How do we find our story ideas?

Unit Goals
- Students will tell stories that contain story elements.
- Students will tell stories that are sequential.
- Students will use strategies for finding story ideas.

Anchor Texts

- *Bedtime for Frances* by Russell Hoban
- *Calabash Cat* by James Rumford
- *Pablo's Tree* by Pat Mora
- *The Paper Bag Princess* by Robert Munsch
- *A Snowy Surprise* by Amy Hest
- *Superhero* by Marc Tauss
- *Tell Me a Story, Mama* by Angela Johnson and David Soman
- *Wilfred Gordon MacDonald Partridge* by Mem Fox
- *William's Doll* by Charlotte Zolotow

Resource Sheets

- Alphabet Chart (Resource 2.1)
- Directions for Making Your Own Story Strings (Resource 2.4)
- Directions for Making Your Own Story Cubes (Resource 2.5)
- Storytelling Homework (Resource 2.6)
- Share a Special Object Homework Assignment (Resource 2.7)
- Paper Samples for Early Fall Units (Resources 2.8–2.11)

Unit Assessment Telling Stories Through Pictures and Words			PROCESS
Student name:	EMERGING	DEVELOPING	INDEPENDENT
Generates story ideas.			
Tells story with proper voice volume and expression.			
Names the "story ingredients" for all stories.			
Includes characters in stories.			
Includes a setting for stories.			
Tells events in a story sequentially.			
Adds print to sketches.			

Stage of the Unit	Focused Instruction You will	Independent Practice Students will
IMMERSION 3 days	• name people whom you like to tell stories to. • name people you love who have told you stories from your own life. • tell both actual events and imagined stories to the students.	• reflect on and sketch whom they like to tell stories to. • reflect on and sketch a storyteller in their life. • tell stories to a partner (real or imagined).
IDENTIFICATION 1 day	• name the "story ingredients" that all stories contain; introduce the Story String for planning and rehearsing stories.	• use Story Strings to plan and rehearse their stories; tell stories to a partner before sketching and/or writing about it.

GUIDED PRACTICE 10 days	• read *Tell Me a Story, Mama* and model how you can use a strong emotion to generate story ideas. • explain how some stories are about topics that are exciting to the author; tell an imagined story that is based on one of the emotions; create a chart of emotions. • model how to add words to your story using an alphabet chart and singing the alphabet song. • use *Wilfrid Gordon MacDonald Partridge* to discuss how authors also find story ideas from objects that are meaningful to them. • read *Pablo's Tree* and discuss what might have inspired author Pat Mora. • model how to be a good listener. • discuss how personal interests can lead to story ideas. Read *Calabash Cat*. • read *Superhero* and discuss how some stories are based on imagination. • model telling a story about a person in the school community, or a story about a class pet or an important object. • use *A Snowy Surprise* to model how authors give characters different voices.	• tell a story to a partner about a time when they felt happy or sad. • use a Story String to develop and sequence their stories. • draw a picture of something special that inspires stories. • use a Story String to practice telling a story to a partner. • draw pictures of things they are interested in. • choose one thing they are interested in and tell a real or imagined story about it. • practice telling a story to a partner and then writing and/or sketching it. • draw objects that are meaningful to them and write the words that go with it above the drawing. • tell a partner a story using the Story String. • practice telling a story to a partner and using a story ingredient from the story to sketch and write about. • change their voice to sound like the different characters when telling their stories to partners.
COMMITMENT 1 day	• guide students through a reflection of their learning in this unit; transcribe the students' reflection statements.	• reflect orally on what they know about telling clear and interesting stories and how using a Story String affects the storytelling process; tell a favorite story to an audience (a friend from the class or another class, older "buddies").
TOTAL: 15 DAYS		

EARLY FALL

LATE FALL

WINTER

SPRING

Kindergarten teacher Janet Knight reflects on story units: "This year my students wrote stories that were longer and more detailed than I had ever encountered before with kindergarteners. Through storytelling, my students were composing stories that were rich and interesting as early as October, when their understanding of letters and sounds were just beginning. By the second half of the year their storytelling muscles were really strong, and their writing skills were beginning to catch up!"

Getting Started

By the time you are ready to begin your work in this unit, your students will be familiar with story elements, or what we refer to as "story ingredients."

Structures and Routines

Partnerships

Children rehearse stories using a Story String. Then they form partnerships and share their stories with one another. When establishing partnerships, consider:

- compatibility—it is still early in the year and you want students to feel comfortable and productive working with one another.

- verbal skills—you may want to create heterogeneous pairs, with more verbally advanced students acting as a model for those who are less so.

- reading partnerships—you may want to use the same partnerships for both reading and writing to simplify routines and establish a comfortable and trusting relationship between students more quickly.

Teaching Materials

Student Materials

The writing folder will house ongoing and completed work. We keep the sketches and writing from this unit. Students can revisit and use their story ideas in subsequent writing units.

Story Strings

A Story String consists of icons glued onto a string to represent the story elements kindergarteners are asked to recognize. You will want to have enough Story Strings for individuals or partnerships to use during the Independent Practice time of this unit. (See Resource 2.4 for directions to make your own.)

Paper Choice

Students will make a sketch each day as a reminder of the story they told. Students choose from blank paper or a page with two lines on the bottom for text. Encourage students who are more fluent at writing to choose the lined paper so they can include a sentence or two that summarizes the story (see Resources 2.8–2.11).

Play Center Connections

Puppet Theater

How many of us have had a puppet theater in our classroom become the miniature stage for the World Wrestling Federation of Puppets? Though students often do not know how to use the puppet theater properly, it can be an effective tool for getting children interested in story. We introduce the puppet theater as a play center after we have begun the story units during reading and writing time. Once it is open, we have available both puppets and familiar picture books for the kids to use in this center. Model for the children how they can use the puppets to retell one of the books in the center or to tell one of their own stories. Talk with students about the story ingredients they've been learning about and help them weave them into their puppet shows. Students can use puppets available in the center or make their own in the art center.

Block Building/Legos

Students create a story to go with a structure they have built and they share this with other play center groups.

Art Center

Students make puppets or familiar books and their own stories for use in the puppet theater.

Story Cubes

Students make cubes that have pictures glued to each side. One cube has character pictures (such as a child, an animal, a wizard, a baby, an alien) and another has setting pictures (jungle, city, farm, outer space). The students roll the cubes and make up a story to go with the character and setting on the cube (see Resource 2.5).

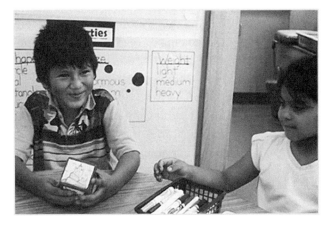

Students have fun telling stories using Story Cubes in a play center.

The Story Chest is another motivating and fun way to engage students in storytelling.

Story Chest

A shoe box serves as a Story Chest containing objects and photographs that the children use to construct a story. A single chest may hold any or all of the following:

- photographs of various settings
- figures to use as the characters (people, animals, imaginary creatures)
- interesting "props" (miniature cars, balls, objects from a dollhouse, bicycles)

Objects are changed regularly so children have a new story experience each time the chest is opened!

Treasure Tells

Once we have studied stories with our students for a couple of weeks, we begin Treasure Tells. The students are asked to bring in an object from home that represents a family story to share with the class. They must be able to tell a story that goes with the object. The story should incorporate the story ingredients.

Stages of the Unit

Immersion

In the beginning of this unit, immerse students in the sound of storytelling. Ask students to think about storytellers in their own lives and to identify the feelings associated with telling and listening to stories. During this time we also invite guest storytellers in to share their family stories or other ones.

Identification

During this lesson, the students reflect on what they have learned about story ingredients in reading time and apply that knowledge to the stories they are telling.

Guided Practice

Introduce the Story Strings in this stage and connect them to what the students already know about story elements. Our students will learn ways to generate ideas for the stories they tell; we read books that help students find story ideas. This stage should contain lots of opportunity for sharing!

Commitment

At the end of this unit we ask students to reflect on what they now know about storytelling. Kindergarteners go through their story sketches from this unit and choose one they would like to tell again in a celebration. Possible celebration ideas include the following:

- Students tell stories to another classmate or a child from another class or grade.
- Pajama Day—children come to school in pajamas and sip hot cocoa while telling stories to one another (this is a scene from the ending of *A Snowy Surprise* by Amy Hest).
- Video- or audiotape student stories.
- Have a "tellabration" and invite families in to sit in small groups and tell stories.

Day-by-Day Lessons

DAY 1 Immersion

Focused Instruction

You all have lots of your own stories to tell. Sometimes the stories we tell are real things that have happened to us and sometimes they are stories are from our imaginations. Think about what kinds of stories you like to tell and who you like to tell your stories to. This person could be someone at home, at school, or maybe even someone you do not see regularly but talk to on the phone. Tell the person next to you what kind of stories you like to tell and who you like to tell them to.

Independent Practice

You are going to draw a picture and write the name of the person or people you like to tell stories to.

- Differentiating Instruction
  - Vulnerable students can add one letter that stands for the name of the person in their drawing.
  - Steady students can write a few letters in the name.
  - Strong students can include information about what kinds of stories they like to tell in addition to the name of the person in their picture.

Wrap-Up

Let's go around now and show our pictures to one another. Say the name of the person in your picture and say what kind of stories you like to tell him or her.

DAY 2 Immersion

Focused Instruction

There are people in my life who are really wonderful storytellers. These people are friends and family who really bring a story to life when they tell it. Do you have a person in your life who tells stories? Someone who may tell you stories about when you were little or maybe someone who tells made-up stories? Tell the person next to you about a storyteller in your life.

Independent Practice

Now you are going to draw a picture of a storyteller in your life and label it with his or her name.

Wrap-Up

Let's go around and say the name of the person you just drew—the storyteller in your life. There are storytellers all around us in school and outside of school. Over the next few days we will have guest storytellers come into our classroom and tell us a story. They will also talk to us about who the storytellers are in their lives and what kind of stories they like to tell—real or imagined.

For a reproducible copy of this homework assignment see Resource 2.6.

DAY 3 Immersion

Focused Instruction

Sometimes I tell stories that are about things that actually happened to me, and other times I like to tell stories I have imagined. I am going to tell you two stories. One is the true story of when I found a praying mantis in my kitchen and the other is an imagined story about a magical praying mantis.

- Tell two stories to your students, one that is an actual event and another that is imagined.

Independent Practice

Now you are going to think of a story to tell your partner. Decide if you want to tell an actual-event story or an imagined one. If you typically tell stories about things that have really happened, try telling an imagined one today.

Wrap-Up

- Have students share whether they told a real story or an imagined story.

DAY 4 Identification

Focused Instruction

You know from our reading unit that there are certain story ingredients we must mix in to make the story clear and easy to understand. Let us name the story ingredients. (Refer to the class chart from reading time.) This object I am holding is a Story String. This string has buttons on it that represent our story ingredients. (Explain the connection between the story ingredients and the buttons.) I will use this Story String to remind myself of the things I need to say when I am telling a story. Today I am going to tell a story about a time when I felt proud of myself.

- Model touching buttons on the string and incorporating that story element into story.

- Make a sketch that represents one key event in the story.

Independent Practice

I have Story Strings for each of you. First you are going to practice saying your story to yourself using your string and then you will meet with your partner and take turns telling your stories. When you are done please make a sketch or write words that show one part of your story.

Wrap-Up

Let's use a Story String, and together we will tell the story of when the bumblebees came into our classroom. That was a time when some of us felt scared, right?

- Tell a story of a shared experience, referring to the story ingredients chart to make sure all story elements are included.

DAY 5 Guided Practice

Focused Instruction

Storytellers tell stories about times that matter to them: funny times, sad times, happy times, angry times. Storytellers think of a strong emotion and recall an experience that went with it. Let me share a memory with you. (Share your memory—your kids will love it!)

- Use *Tell Me a Story, Mama,* and discuss how strong emotions go along with great stories.

Independent Practice

Think of a time when you felt happy or sad or angry or a time that was funny. Remember the story that goes with that emotion. Then you will meet with your partner and take turns telling your stories.

Wrap-Up

Let's write down a list of different emotions we have all had. Thinking about an emotion will remind us of stories we can tell.

- Chart emotions, using sketches that correspond with the items on the chart.

Students using Story Strings, which help them develop and sequence their stories.

DAY 6 Guided Practice

Focused Instruction

Yesterday you found story ideas by thinking of a time when you felt a certain emotion. You told stories of things that actually happened. Today I am going to show you how to use our list of emotions to think of an imagined story.

One word on our chart is "excited." I want to imagine a story about this emotion. Flying carpets, unicorns, and magical items are all make-believe and would be very exciting to me. I am going to make up a story about riding on a flying carpet.

- Tell an imagined story based on an emotion from the chart.

Now I am going to make a quick sketch and add some words to remind myself of this story.

- Make a sketch and add a few words that are key to the story.

Independent Practice

Now you are going to use the emotion chart to think of a story you want to tell to your partner today. The story can be real or imagined. After you have told your story, you will make a sketch of one part of it.

- Differentiating Instruction
  - Strong writers can write sentences to accompany sketches.

Wrap-Up

- Ask one or two students to tell their story to the class.

Thinking of an emotion helps students to generate story ideas independently.

DAY 7 Guided Practice

Focused Instruction

You have been making a sketch of one part of your story so you can remember it later. Today you are going to add words to your story sketches. Your alphabet chart can help you to add the words you are looking for. Here is a sketch that shows one part of my flying carpet story I told you yesterday. I want to add the words "carpet" and "sky" because those words are important to the story. Let me say the word "carpet" very closely and listen for the first sound.

- Model using pictures on the chart to identify the letter that makes a particular sound.
- Model locating a particular letter on the chart by singing the alphabet song and pointing to the letters as you sing them until you get to the letter you are looking for.

Independent Practice

Plan out a story to tell your partner using a Story String. After partnerships have finished storytelling, talk about the sketch you will make. Tell your partner what two words you will add to your sketch. Remember that your alphabet chart can help you to find letters you need for your writing.

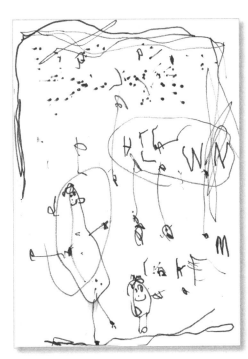

A vulnerable writer draws a picture that represents a Halloween story she told. She uses an alphabet chart to add letters to the picture.

A strong writer writes the ending of her story: "And then the sun came out and the princess played outside."

- Differentiating Instruction
  - Strong writers can write a sentence or two to accompany their sketch.
  - Vulnerable writers can write a few letters copied from the alphabet chart to accompany sketch.
- Confer with students and small groups. Record the words students are writing on their sketches to share during Wrap-Up.

Wrap-Up

Listen to some of the words your classmates have added to their sketches.

DAY 8 Guided Practice

Focused Instruction

Storytellers find the ideas for their stories in different places. We read Wilfrid Gordon McDonald Partridge *the other day. In this book Wilfrid helped Miss Nancy remember stories from her life by showing her objects like the egg and the puppet. Today I brought in something to share with you. This is a special dish my grandmother used for her holiday cookies. Listen as I tell you a story about making holiday cookies with my grandmother.*

- Bring in an object of significance to share with students. Tell a story that goes with the object.

Think about some special objects you have at home—like the objects Wilfrid brought to Miss Nancy or my holiday dish. Think, turn, and tell the person next to you about a few of your special things.

Independent Practice

Now you will draw pictures of some of the special things that inspire stories for you. Be sure to label your pictures.

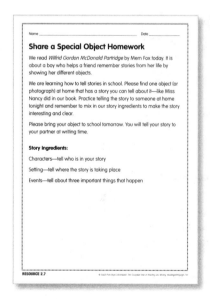

RESOURCE 2.7

Wrap-Up

Bring your pictures to the meeting area. Share your drawings with the person sitting next to you.

- Read *William's Doll*. Discuss Charlotte Zolotow's inspiration for the story.
- Distribute "Share a Special Object" homework assignment. See Resource 2.7.

DAY 9 Guided Practice

Focused Instruction

Here is a book we know, Pablo's Tree *by Pat Mora. As we read the book think aloud how the object that is very important to Pablo is the little tree, because it reminds him of his adoption story.*

- Revisit a portion of the story that refers to the importance of the tree.

You all have objects from home with you. Think about the story you will tell that goes with it.

Independent Practice

First you will practice telling your story with a Story String. Then you will meet with your partner and take turns telling your stories. After that, you will make a sketch of one part of your story. The writing you add to your sketches today will be about the object in your story.

Wrap-Up

Was thinking about a special object helpful in finding an idea for a story to tell?

- Students put their special objects out on a table and then walk around to look at each other's objects.

DAY 10 Guided Practice

Focused Instruction

When your partner is telling a story to you during Independent Practice, you are the audience. One of your jobs as the audience for your partner is to listen carefully for our story ingredients. Another job the audience has is to make eye contact with the storyteller. Watch me make eye contact with Kareem. Eye contact helps you to listen closely. Watch as I turn my whole body to Kareem—this helps me to make eye contact and listen to his story.

Decide on the story you want to tell today. Use the emotion chart or your special object to think of a story if you are stuck.

Independent Practice

Once you have your story idea, please get a Story String and practice telling your story. When you meet to share your story with your partner, remember to turn your bodies toward each other and to make eye contact.

Today the sketches you make about your story and the words you add will be about the ending of your story.

Wrap-Up

- Share the writing that a few students included on their sketches.

DAY 11 Guided Practice

Focused Instruction

We have been talking about how storytellers get the ideas for their stories. We know that thinking about an emotion and objects that have special meaning for us are two ways to find ideas for stories. Today I am sharing with you one more strategy for finding story ideas—things you are interested in. Watch me as I make sketches of things I am interested in. These will give me ideas for the stories I want to tell.

- Make a list of interests that could inspire ideas for stories. For example: gardening, mountain biking, Harry Potter, magic, and sailing.

What are things you are interested in? Think, turn, and tell the person next to you.

- Shares a few student examples to generate ideas for other children.

Independent Practice

You will use the paper with boxes on it to draw a picture of things you are interested in. For each thing, write the word to go with it somewhere in the box.

Wrap-Up

- Have students share their list with a partner. Post the papers in the room so students can look at each other's lists throughout the day.
- Read *Calabash Cat* and discuss where students think James Rumford found his inspiration.

DAY 12 Guided Practice

Focused Instruction

Some of the stories I have been hearing you tell are about things that have actually happened to you. Others are telling imaginary stories. Yesterday you made sketches of things that you are interested in and today you are going to tell a story about something on your list. Two of my interests are sailing and Harry Potter. Listen as I make up a story about a magic boat that takes me to places around the world.

- Model telling an imaginary story based on your interests.

Independent Practice

Look at the list of things you are interested in and choose one to tell a story about. It can be a real or an imaginary story. Once you have the idea in your head, practice telling it on a Story String and then tell it to your partner. Make a sketch and write about an important event in your story—one thing that happened.

Wrap-Up

- Share a few examples of student work. There should be a range of samples from vulnerable to strong students. Highlight some aspect of the work: the story idea, the sketch, or the writing.
- Read *Superhero* and discuss how some stories are imaginary.

DAY 13 Guided Practice

Focused Instruction

Together we are going to tell a story about our class pet, Clarence the goldfish.

- Choose an important object, class pet, or person in the school community about which to tell a story.
- Help facilitate the telling of a story, either real or imagined. Draw students' attention to the story ingredients that help you sequence your story.

Independent Practice

Once you have decided on your story idea, you may go off to practice it then tell it to your partner. Today you may choose a story ingredient from your story that you would like to sketch and write about.

Wrap-Up

- If the students told a real story in the Focused Instruction, tell an imaginary one based on the same subject.

DAY 14 Guided Practice

Focused Instruction

When you tell stories through pictures in books, you practice using a voice that sounds like the characters. When you get to a point in A Snowy Surprise *when Mrs. Bear is talking, you use a voice that sounds like a mom. When Sam is talking, you use a kid voice. When you tell your own stories you can also use different voices that sound like different characters. This can make your story interesting and fun to listen to. Listen to me as I tell you a real story and use different voices for different people in my story.*

- Model telling a story using different voices for the characters.

Independent Practice

When you tell your story today, try changing your voice to sound like the different characters in your story. Then make a sketch and add words that tell the ending of your story.

- Confer and/or work with small groups of students. Look for students who use interesting character voices in their stories that would serve as good examples to highlight in the Wrap-Up.

Wrap-Up

- Ask a few of the students to tell a part of their stories where they used character voices.

DAY 15 Commitment

Focused Instruction

Today is the last day of our unit on storytelling. We are going to reflect on what we have learned about the stories we tell to others. Think about the stories you are telling now and the stories you used to tell before we started this study. How are your stories different? Think, turn, and tell the person sitting next to you.

- Record student responses—these may be displayed on sentence strips or chart paper.

Independent Practice

Look through the sketches you made of the stories you told over the past few weeks. Choose one story that you particularly like. What do you like about it? Think, turn, and tell the person sitting next to you. I am going to pass out new markers and you can add details and color to this sketch. This is the story you will tell again in our storytelling celebration.

Wrap-Up

- Have a storytelling celebration! Students meet in small groups to take turns telling each other their favorite story. For example, the last scene in *Snowy Surprise* by Amy Hest features the characters Mrs. Bear and Sam telling stories to each other while drinking hot cocoa and wearing cozy socks. Kindergarten teacher Nicole Viscomi celebrates this unit in the spirit of *Snowy Surprise*. Her students wear their favorite pajamas and bring in a teddy bear to school. Nicole provides hot cocoa for the children as they meet in small groups to tell stories to one another.

All the World Is Play

The next units in reading and writing are about connecting print and literacy to each other in the spirit of building and creating and play. For the kindergarten student, much of life is about building and creating. Recently on a trip to South Africa, we watched as children in a small rural village made a house out of a box. For the next two hours, while we sat and listened, they created worlds of stories out of that box. Children will find many ways to open doors to play. It is as essential to them as air itself, which is why we use play in these units to foster literacy development. In recent years, there has been some polarization regarding those teachers who feel strongly connected to the idea of play in the kindergarten classroom and others who feel school must be purely "academic."

In Susan Kempton's book *The Literate Kindergarten* (2007), she writes: "When I say play, I am not talking just about recreation and fun. In a broader sense, play encompasses all sorts of sensory-based environments where children can explore and interact, both with others and with a variety of materials. In these environments, children are most themselves. Play is their natural language and thus the best way to see their learning process."

Also, let's not forget this: play is fun, and it is a deep human desire for connectedness and imagination that creates strong communities and provides sustenance to growing minds. We hope this book makes a strong case for blending play and active engagement with literacy. Stuart Brown, president of the National Institute for Play, recently said that play is part of "the developmental sequencing of becoming a human primate. If you look at what produces learning and memory and well-being, play is as fundamental as any other aspect of life, including sleep and dreams."

Reading for Many Purposes: Connecting Books to Play

PROCESS

Why Teach This?

- To show students the connections they can make from books to their imagined lives.
- To help students understand that books can travel with them into different dimensions of their lives.
- To help students use known stories to create new ones.

Framing Question

- How can we use our favorite books in our play centers?

Unit Goals

- Students will use books to enhance play.
- Students will use stories in books to develop stories in their play.
- Students will incorporate information from books into play.

Anchor Texts

- *Castle* by David McCauley
- Walt Disney's *Cinderella*
- *Madlenka* by Peter Sis
- *Whistle for Willie* by Ezra Jack Keats

Unit Assessment Reading for Many Purposes: Connecting Books to Play			PROCESS
Student name:	EMERGING	DEVELOPING	INDEPENDENT
Integrates known stories into play.			
Uses information (characters, setting, plot, events) from books to enhance play.			
Uses visual images or story settings to inspire play.			
Uses books to tell stories in play.			

Stage of the Unit	Focused Instruction You will	Independent Practice Students will
IMMERSION 1 day	• read aloud from *Madlenka* and model for students how to plan what they might do with their story as they play.	• choose one part of *Madlenka* and try to incorporate it into their play. (For example, pretend to be Madlenka as she visits all her friends.)

IDENTIFICATION 1 day	• read aloud from *Whistle for Willie* and identify different ways readers use books in their play:
	  • They adapt stories and use the ideas in their play.
	  • They use the pictures or the photos to create structures in blocks or with legos.
	  • They use books as props as they role-play various ways readers use books in their lives (using cookbooks in the kitchen, tucking a baby in to bed with a goodnight story).
		• take one book from the classroom library and choose how they will use their book during playtime.

GUIDED PRACTICE 2 days	• demonstrate how students might use *Castle* by David McCauley during their playtime: building castles, for example. • demonstrate how you might use *Cinderella* in play: acting out a scene or retelling the story.	• select and read books in partnerships to use in playtime: either to build from or to tell stories from in play groups. • discuss in partnerships how they will use their book and then proceed to a center.
COMMITMENT 1 day	• reflect on different ways children used stories and books to build and construct play ideas.	• share examples of how they used books to support their play. • visit one another's play areas to see how books were incorporated.
TOTAL: 5 DAYS		

Plays on Words

While in their play areas, kindergarteners are busy with the work of their imagined lives. During writing time, they are busy making things for the world to see. Their writing ties into their imaginative play and serves the same purposes: fostering communication, generating ideas, and developing strategies for how we express ideas to one another on the deepest level. Let's journey now into writing time to see how play can inform and inspire the written form.

Writing for Many Purposes: Connecting Writing to Play

PROCESS

Why Teach This?

- To show students the connections they can make from their writing to their imagined lives.
- To help students understand that writing has a purpose in different dimensions of their lives.
- To develop students' genre awareness.

Framing Questions

- What are different kinds of writing?

Unit Goals

- Students will write a letter or a song to someone they care about.
- Students will write labels and signs in play centers and around the room.
- Students will make lists that have real purpose.

Anchor Texts

- *Fancy Nancy* by Robin Preiss Glasser
- *Frog and Toad Together* by Arnold Lobel
- *I Wanna Iguana* by Karen Kaufman Orloff
- *The Jolly Postman* by Allan Ahlberg
- *Signs in Our World* by DK Publishing
- *What a Wonderful World* by Bob Thiele

Unit Assessment Writing for Many Purposes: Connecting Writing to Play			PROCESS
Student name:	EMERGING	DEVELOPING	INDEPENDENT
Incorporates writing into play activities.			
Writes letters and/or songs.			
Engages in list writing during play activities.			
Creates signs for play or authentic purposes.			

Stage of the Unit	Focused Instruction You will	Independent Practice Students will
IMMERSION 2 days	• read *Fancy Nancy*; explore the different ways Nancy uses writing (lists, signs, labels). • read *What a Wonderful World*; discuss song writers as authors.	• think of a way to use writing and drawing (lists, signs, labels) in their play centers (play centers include dramatic play, housekeeping, blocks, art center). • be open to the idea of creating songs to accompany their play.

IDENTIFICATION
1 day
	• identify different ways writers use writing in their play:
	  • they draw and write labels for block structures, items of importance in various centers;
	  • they draw and write signs (e.g., to communicate warnings or important information);
	  • they draw and write lists (e.g., for the housekeeping center—grocery list, to-do list);
	  • they draw and write letters or notes (e.g., for the class mailbox, family members).
		• make a paper choice (list paper, sticky note, index card, blank paper) to bring into a play center and incorporate writing into their play.

GUIDED PRACTICE 3 days	• read *Signs in Our World*; imagine purposes for signs in different centers. • read *The Jolly Postman* and introduce the class mailbox; have students write letters to classmates or others in the school (two students can be mail carriers and deliver any mail students write). (Alternate text: *I Wanna Iguana*; consider creating a post office in one of the play centers.) • read the story "The List" from *Frog and Toad Together*; imagine purposes for list writing in different centers.	• include writing in their play (letter writing in the writing center is one choice the students may make). • see possibilities for list writing in different play centers.
COMMITMENT 1 day	• reflect on and celebrate the different ways children used writing to build and construct play ideas (have a play center celebration by touring each other's play areas and complimenting them).	• visit one another's play centers to see how writing and drawing were incorporated.
TOTAL: 7 DAYS		

From Early Fall to Late Fall

Your kindergarteners have been imagining worlds of stories and finding ways to get to know each other through literacy via play and print. The room is alive with the buzz of words and stories; there is laughter in the air, and a sense of the possibilities—everyone will learn how to read! The next season will bring with it units in reading words and writing them, all without worry or fear, as well as an introduction to genres and to the potential talk has to deepen thinking. Your classroom is a cozy hub of learning.

Chapter 3

LATE FALL

The Kindergartener as Word Builder

"We're ready to work, and our tools are ready, too."
—from *Growing Vegetable Soup* by Lois Ehlert

For the kindergartener, work and play are one and the same. He puts on his pretend tool belt, gets his building blocks in order, and sets out to build new worlds or words from a combination of his imagination and the real world around him. During this season, we will share units of study about how to read and write words with confidence as well as how our youngest readers and writers can make wise and successful choices as they become more independent. Join us as we take you on a tour of these late fall units of study designed to give your kindergarteners the tools they need for lifelong success in literacy.

LATE FALL UNITS

- Reading Words With Confidence: Using Decoding Strategies, *page 64*
- Writing Words Without Worry: Using Spelling Strategies, *page 74*

SPOTLIGHT UNITS

- Deepening Capacity for Talk: Reading Partnerships, *page 84*
- Deepening Capacity for Talk: Writing Partnerships, *page 86*
- Exploring the World of Genres: A Reading Unit, *page 88*
- Exploring the World of Genres: A Writing Unit, *page 90*
- Making Choices as Readers, *page 92*
- Making Choices as Writers: The Four Prompts, *page 94*

SPOTLIGHT on Conventions

- Reading Words With Confidence: Using Decoding Strategies
- Writing Words Without Worry: Using Spelling Strategies

As kindergarten teachers, we often either dread the teaching of conventions because they feel so detached from the liveliness of our students' literacy experiences or we cram in lots of instruction in concentrated periods of time, worried that we are not covering it all before they move on to the next grade. The Complete 4 approach advocates finding a middle ground. We are not going to teach conventions in isolation (although we do advocate regular word work time for practice with patterns and strategies), nor are we going to ignore them. Instead, we are going to carefully place conventions instruction where it belongs: alongside students' authentic work. We celebrate language, punctuation, and grammar in ways that respect and give dignity to the way kindergarteners are coming to print. The writer Eudora Welty recalled her first glimpse, as a child, of the alphabet inside her storybooks and how magical the swirls and curves of each letter seemed. Let us capture that magic in units on conventions. See page 62 to 72 in *The Complete 4 for Literacy* for more guidelines for this component.

Pam Allyn

We Are Word Builders

The kindergartener is coming into her own. She is beginning to "feel her oats." More comfortable with routines, she may be ready for some new ones. She is curious about her new friends and what they are doing during reading and writing time. She is better able to construct long-term thinking about her ideas. She wants to unlock the secrets of print. The time is ripe for units on conventions and partnership opportunities where more structured work is done to build collaboration and foster skills in conversation about writing, both their own and that of others. We track back now to narrative reading and writing, this time adding layers upon our first forays in early fall, strengthening our students' knowledge of story elements and giving them the opportunity to use their oral storytelling abilities as a vehicle to becoming fluent writers.

Reading Words With Confidence: Using Decoding Strategies

CONVENTIONS

Why Teach This?

- To enable students to apply their knowledge of sounds and symbols to decode unknown words.
- To teach students multiple cueing systems in reading (semantics, syntax, grapho-phonemic).
- To teach students to collaborate as a way to work through difficulties.

Framing Question

- What strategies can we use to tackle difficult words?

Unit Goals

- Students will use their knowledge of letters and sounds to read unknown words.
- Students will use context and syntax clues to read unknown words.
- Students will use multiple cueing systems when attempting to read unknown words.

Anchor Texts

- *The Big Book of Words for Curious Kids* by Heloise Antoine
- *Cassie's Word Quilt* by Faith Ringgold
- *First the Egg* by Laura Vaccaro Seeger
- *Garden Friends* by DK Publishing
- *Growing Vegetable Soup* by Lois Ehlert
- *Jack's Garden* by Henry Cole
- *My First Body Board Book: Spanish/English* by DK Publishing
- *My First Farm Board Book: Spanish/English* by DK Publishing
- *My First Word Book* by DK Publishing
- *Snowballs* by Lois Ehlert
- *Tools* by Taro Miura
- *Vegetables* by Sara Andersen

Resource Sheets

- Parent Letter (Resource 3.1)
- Labeling Homework (Resource 3.2)
- Paper Samples (Resources 3.3–3.6)

Unit Assessment Reading Words With Confidence: Using Decoding Strategies			CONVENTIONS
Student name:	EMERGING	DEVELOPING	INDEPENDENT
Locates and writes labels.			
Uses picture clues to read new words.			
Uses knowledge of letter sounds to read new words.			
Uses meaning to confirm or revise reading.			
Applies multiple strategies to read new words.			

Stage of the Unit	Focused Instruction You will	Independent Practice Students will
IMMERSION 2 days	• read *Cassie's Word Quilt* and celebrate the labels students know how to read in the classroom. • introduce books with labels to students.	• make labels for additional objects in the classroom. • browse books, looking for labels and attempting to read them.
IDENTIFICATION 1 day	• read *Tools* by Taro Miura and name the strategies a reader uses to read difficult words. • make the analogy that being a smart reader is like being a detective.	• reflect on their process when encountering a hard word; mark difficult words they were able to decode successfully.
GUIDED PRACTICE 6 days	• read *Vegetables* by Sara Andersen and demonstrate using picture clues to read an unknown word. • use *My First Body Board Book* to demonstrate using the first letter of an unknown word and the picture to figure it out. • demonstrate how rereading and checking for meaning helps readers figure out hard words.	• use picture clues to read an unknown word. • study beginning letters and pictures to read unknown words. • reread and check for meaning when figuring out hard words.

GUIDED PRACTICE *(continued)*	• read *First the Egg* and demonstrate how good readers cross-check for meaning while they read. • demonstrate stretching the sounds in a hard word.	• begin to ask, "Does this word make sense?" to check for meaning during reading. • stretch the sounds in hard words.
COMMITMENT 1 day	• guide students through a reflection of what they've learned in this unit.	• orally reflect on how they have grown as readers; make bookmarks that list reading moves to figure out unknown words.

TOTAL: 10 DAYS

Getting Started

Gather a number of books with pictures that are labeled and form partnerships before beginning this unit. Students will begin this unit focused on these label books, but will progress into decoding words in other fiction and nonfiction books. Reflect back to the books students brought with them into play centers during the previous unit. Partnerships are ability-based, so formal and/or informal assessments of students' understanding of letters and sounds should be completed before you begin this conventions unit.

Structures and Routines
Partnerships

In this unit we are forming ability-based partnerships. Students read independently for 10 to 15 minutes followed by 10 minutes of partner time. Partnerships read words to one another from their books and ask for help with words that have proven too difficult to decode independently. Place two to three partnerships of similar ability at one table and provide them with a basket of books.

Teaching Materials

In this unit you will demonstrate how thoughtful readers use information from pictures, letters, and context to successfully decode tricky words. This type of instruction is best done with enlarged text, although it is not essential. In the beginning of this unit, our focus is on label books. By the end of the unit, you can expand your focus to include decoding hard words in fiction and nonfiction books. Two of our favorite label books include *Cassie's Word Quilt* by Faith Ringgold and *Tools* by Taro Miura.

Choosing the Labeled Texts for Students to Read

We have discovered two styles of label books: one is constructed of pictures, organized by topic, with a single label naming the object. The most common form is the baby word book, such as *Baby's First 50 Words*.

The other type of label book has a main body of text (narrative or informational) with labeled pictures as an added feature. Authors such as Lois Ehlert and Gail Gibbons often use labeled pictures in their books.

Differentiation

Teaching print strategies inside label books gives us the ability to differentiate instruction for all of our students. By focusing on labels initially, a kindergartener can focus his energies on a single word. He can practice specific strategies and focus on a handful of letters in isolation rather than their being surrounded by many new and challenging words. Any label book may have words appropriate for our vulnerable students as well as words for our strongest students. In *Garden Friends* by DK Publishing, you will find the label "wing" as well as "antenna." A label is nonthreatening for our vulnerable students. Our ELL students are well served reading label books, as they help to expand their vocabulary. By moving them forward from labels to fiction and nonfiction books, we give students the opportunity to practice strategies on a variety of hard words in a variety of texts. This strengthens their ability to decode hard words in any book they choose.

Below, we have listed label books by some favorite authors that feel especially appropriate for each category of reader. Publishers such as Rigby Wright Group and Scholastic often have labeled books in their earliest leveled guided reading sets.

Vulnerable Readers

- *At the Beach* (Kingfisher Board Books) by Mandy Stanley
- *Busy Bugs* (Kingfisher Board Books) by Mandy Stanley
- *First Word Book* by Mandy Stanley
- *I Read Signs* by Tana Hoban
- *My School Day* by Lee Scott, National Geographic (big book)
- *Signs in Our World* by DK Publishing
- *Vegetables* by Sara Anderson

Steady Readers

- *Doll and Teddy* (The Baby's Catalogue Series) by Janet Ahlberg
- *First 100 Animals* (First Words) by Roger Priddy
- *Garden Friends* by DK Readers
- *Growing Vegetable Soup* by Lois Ehlert
- *Meet the Dinosaurs* by DK Readers
- *Nuts to You* by Lois Ehlert
- *A Year in the Country* by Douglas Florian

Strong Readers

- *Dinosaur ABC* by Roger Priddy
- *Dogs* by Gail Gibbons
- *Ice Cream: The Full Scoop* by Gail Gibbons
- *Fire! Fire!* by Gail Gibbons

- *Knights in Shining Armor* by Gail Gibbons
- *My Big Truck Book* by Roger Priddy
- *Thanksgiving Is...* by Gail Gibbons
- *Waiting for Wings* by Lois Ehlert

Stages of the Unit

Immersion

Students explore the purposes of labels in the classroom and in books. Kindergarteners reflect on what they currently do when they encounter unknown words in books. A parent letter can be sent home at this time (see Resource 3.1).

Identification

A class chart is made that lists what a student can do to read an unknown word. Sketches are made to represent each strategy so students can easily access the information. Items on the chart should include look at the picture, look at the letters, think about what would make sense.

Guided Practice

In this stage, you demonstrate finding clues to decode an unknown word: picture clues, letter clues, and meaning. Students read independently then talk with partners about words they've successfully decoded as well as those that remain a mystery.

Commitment

Students make bookmarks with sketches representing different reading strategies (from the class chart). To celebrate the learning in this unit, students choose a favorite book and read it with a friend.

Day-by-Day Lessons

DAY 1 Immersion

Focused Instruction

In this unit, we are going to celebrate words! We are going to find them everywhere and have small celebrations every time we can read them. Have you seen words around you that you realize you can read on your own? Let's look around our classroom and find words we know.

- Students read labels with the names of classmates in various locations throughout the room. Students find and read other labels in the classroom.

You all found words you could read in our room. Today you are going to find an object in the room and make a label for it. Labels are like little signs that tell someone what something is.

- Model making a label for an object in the classroom.

Independent Practice

Everyone has an index card. Find an object in the room with your partner and make a label for it. Say the word slowly and write the letters you hear.

Wrap-Up

- Students share with the class the labels they wrote and then display the labels next to the objects.

DAY 2 Immersion

Focused Instruction

There are many books that have labels in them, and today you will find some in your book baskets. Here is one called Vegetables *by Sara Anderson. I am going to read this book today looking for labels. When I find one, I am going to see if I can read it.*

- Model reading the book, thinking aloud about the pictures, pointing out labels, and trying to read them.

Independent Practice

Today during Independent Practice you will browse through the books in your basket. Try to find the labels in the book and see if you can read them. After that you will have time to work with your partner.

- Students read independently.

Choose one book you would like to share with your partner. Tell your partner why you are choosing that particular book: perhaps you liked the pictures or the topic of the book really interests you. Then you can look through the book together. See if you can read the labels with your partner.

Wrap-Up

- Share homework with the students (see Resource 3.2).

DAY 3 Identification

Focused Instruction

When we are reading, there are some words that we know right away. But then there are many other words that we do not know. Sometimes these words are tricky and we must really work hard to figure out what they say. Today we are going to talk about strategies that good readers use to figure out hard words, not just labels, but any hard words in their books.

- Make a chart that lists strategies students can use to read unfamiliar words.

- Create a sketch to represent each strategy on the chart.
- Possible items on the chart:
  - Look at the pictures on the page.
  - Look at the letters in the word.
  - Think about what would make sense.

Independent Practice

When you are reading your books today, pay attention to the strategies you use to read new or tricky words. When it is partner reading time, talk about what you did to read these words. See if you and your partner can use one of the strategies on our chart to figure out a word you do not know.

Wrap-Up

We are going to go around the room so everyone can share a word they read today that made them proud.

DAY 4 Guided Practice

Focused Instruction

Looking for clues to read tricky words is a lot like being a detective. Detectives find clues that help them to solve mysteries. Readers find clues to figure out words they do not know...mystery words!

- Reinforce word-attack strategies from Day 3 with a new text, modeling what it means to look for clues on a page. Also model using a sticky note to mark a word that you solved by finding clues on the page.

Independent Practice

If you get stuck on a tricky word, remember to look for clues around the page that may help you to solve that mystery word. Everyone will get one sticky note. If you were able to solve a mystery word by finding clues, mark it with a note. At partner time read the word and tell what clues you found that enabled you to solve the mystery.

- After 10 minutes of independent reading, the students meet with partners.

Wrap-Up

Who read a tricky word today by finding clues on the page? Where did you find the clues? Is there anything else we should add to our chart?

DAY 5 Guided Practice

Focused Instruction

You can figure out challenging words by looking at the pictures. In some books, the pictures match the words. Let us look at the words on the first page of the book Growing Vegetable Soup. *We will do some detective work to find clues in the pictures that will help us to read the tricky words.*

- Use an enlarged text to model using picture clues to read an unknown word.

Today you will use two sticky notes, one to mark a tricky word you figured out and one to mark one that is still a mystery.

- Model using the two sticky notes on one page of the enlarged text.

Independent Practice

Everyone will get two sticky notes; one is for a word you were stuck on but then found clues that helped you to read it. The other note is for a word that is still a mystery. At partner reading time, you will share the two words you marked. Together, see if you and your partner can find clues to read the mystery word.

- Differentiating Instruction
  - Strong readers should be encouraged to read all the words in their book smoothly and fluently. Picture clues will help them read unfamiliar words.

Wrap-Up

- Choose two students to share the work they did with picture clues and reading labels.

DAY 6 Guided Practice

Focused Instruction

Whenever you read a book, you can look at the pictures for clues to help you read the words. Today we are also going to look at the first letter of a hard word, a mystery word, and the picture to see if it will help us read the word. In the book Cassie's Word Quilt, *I see that there is something that looks like a blanket in the picture. But the hard word starts with a "Q," so the word can't be "blanket."*

- Think aloud about what this hard word could be, going through a mental list of words it could or couldn't be.

This word is "quilt." I know that is a kind of a blanket. Did you see how I looked at the first letter in the word and the picture to try to figure it out?

Independent Practice

Today when you are reading, look carefully at the first letter in your hard word. What sound does that letter make? Use your alphabet charts to help you.

- Differentiating Instruction
  - Strong readers can look for chunks of familiar letters inside of longer words.
- Reading partners share the words they were able to successfully decode and then help one another with the words they were unable to read independently.

Wrap-Up

- Choose a pair of students to share their work with pictures, letters, and letter sounds.

DAY 7 Guided Practice

Focused Instruction

Yesterday we practiced looking at the first letter and the picture to help us figure out a word we do not know, a mystery word. Another strategy that good readers use is to reread the sentence with the hard word and stop at the mystery word. Then look at the first letter and picture to figure out what the word might be. Reread the sentence to see if the meaning you've come up with makes sense.

- Model getting stuck on a hard word, reread it once, look at the first letter and the picture to figure out what the word is, and then reread the sentence as a whole.

Did you notice how many times I read the sentence? It is important to reread the sentence to figure out what the word might be.

Independent Practice

Today if you get stuck on a hard word, you will reread the sentence a bunch of times before and after you figure out the word. Make sure the word you figured out makes sense in the sentence.

Wrap-Up

- Choose a partnership to share the reading work it did by using picture and letter clues and rereading.

DAY 8 Guided Practice

Focused Instruction

As reading detectives, you have been looking at pictures and letters to find clues that help you to solve mystery words. When detectives are gathering their clues, they stop and ask themselves, "Does this make sense?" Here is our book, Growing Vegetable Soup. *I am going to work on a mystery word.*

- Demonstrate using picture and letter strategies to figure out a hard word, including rereading the sentence numerous times. At the end of the page, think aloud to check in on whether the meaning of the story is making sense.

Independent Practice

Today when you are gathering clues, remember to stop and ask yourself, "Does this make sense?" When you meet with your partner, you will share clues you found for a hard word and your thinking about what did and did not make sense.

Wrap-Up

- Have the whole class practice looking at picture and letter clues in a book and cross-checking for meaning.

DAY 9 Guided Practice

Focused Instruction

Today we are going to go beyond the first letter to the other letters in a mystery word. We can stretch sounds in a word. Let me show you how I do that.

- Model stretching the sounds in various hard words from a read-aloud or big book.

Independent Practice

Today when you work on mystery words in your books or tricky labels, look beyond the first letter. Look for other letters you know that may help you to read the word. Stretch the sounds in the word. Remember to use your alphabet chart if you need it.

- Differentiating Instruction
  - Vulnerable readers can focus on initial consonants in labels.
  - Steady readers may be looking at initial and ending consonants.
  - Strong readers can identify words.

Wrap-Up

When I met with some of you during independent practice, I saw smart detective work.

- Highlight the work of two or three students.

DAY 10 Commitment

Focused Instruction

Today is the last day of our unit. We are going to take a minute to reflect on what we have learned. What can you do as a reader now that you could not do before this unit? How is being a reader like being a detective? Where can you look for clues that will help you to read words in your book? What can you do if you are stuck on a word?

- Students share their reflections with one another.
- Record students' reflections to be displayed or filed in student assessment records.

Independent Practice

To remind yourself of all you have learned in this unit, you will make a bookmark. On the bookmark you will draw pictures of what you can do to figure out and read a mystery word. You will be drawing the same pictures that we have on our class chart.

Wrap-Up

Celebrate the learning in this unit! Students write a few words that they are proud they can read independently on index cards or sentence strips. These words are displayed on a bulletin board along with the students' reflections on the unit.

Reading Mystery Words

Look at the picture.

Look at the letters in the word.

Think about what would make sense.

Conventions bookmarks are a celebration and a reminder of what to do when stuck on a new word.

Print Matters

We recall Allison, age six. In the later part of the year, we asked her what she felt she had learned most as a writer, and she said proudly: "I used to think a W was actually a D, because the W is called a "double-u" and it sounds like a D! I grew the most as a writer in this way—learning what a W is actually for!" We were delighted by Allison's pride in her achievement. It seemed to sum up so much of the life and spirit of the kindergartener— how new the world is for them! How new and how glorious those shapes of letters are, and the sounds they make. Embrace the study of conventions with our youngest writers: it is all new to them, and all an exciting journey of discovery and adventure.

Yet the prospect of spelling an unfamiliar, multisyllabic word can stop a kindergartener in his tracks! In this unit, we teach specific strategies for spelling unknown words, giving our kindergarteners a sense of control over their words.

Writing Words Without Worry: Using Spelling Strategies

CONVENTIONS

Why Teach This?
- To teach students specific strategies for spelling unknown words.
- To give students the confidence to spell words to the best of their ability.
- To encourage students to take risks and expand their writing vocabulary.

Framing Question
- What can we do when we want to spell a new word in our writing?

Unit Goals
- Students will use their knowledge of letters and sounds to spell words.
- Students will use spelling resources available to them to spell words.
- Students will spell words confidently and independently.

Anchor Texts
- *Cassie's Word Quilt* by Faith Ringgold
- *First Word Book* by Mandy Stanley
- *My Big Truck Book* by Roger Priddy
- *Vegetables* by Sara Anderson

Resource Sheets
- Paper Choices (Resources 3.3–3.6)

Unit Assessment Writing Words Without Worry: Using Spelling Strategies			CONVENTIONS
Student name:	EMERGING	DEVELOPING	INDEPENDENT
Uses sound spelling to write new words.			
Uses spelling resources to write new words.			
Uses sight spelling to write new words.			
Attempts to spell new words with confidence.			
Writes independently.			

Stage of the Unit	Focused Instruction You will	Independent Practice Students will
IMMERSION 4 days	• point out labels in the classroom and discuss their purpose. • discuss current knowledge students possess about labels in books and their purpose. • demonstrate finding writing ideas by thinking of a favorite book; revisit *Cassie's Word Quilt* and *My Big Truck Book*.	• write a label for an object in their play center. • sketch a picture that tells a story and label it. • explore label books from their reading to inspire the writing of their own books.
IDENTIFICATION 1 day	• read *First Word Book* and identify what writers do when they want to spell a new word.	• write label books using spelling strategies shared in the Focused Instruction; spy on themselves as they spell new words and add any new strategies to the class chart.
GUIDED PRACTICE 5 days	• demonstrate using the sound strategy for spelling on dry-erase boards. • demonstrate using an alphabet chart as a spelling resource. • analyze how information is organized in *My Big Truck Book*. This gives students a model for writing and organizing their own label books. • demonstrate using the sight strategy for spelling with dry-erase boards. • introduce class mantra "Don't worry, keep going" to encourage children to press on when unsure about the spelling of words.	• use the sound strategy when spelling new words. • use alphabet charts when spelling new words. • write label books with an awareness of organizational structure. • try to use the sight strategy when spelling new words. • attempt to use new and interesting words in their writing without the worry of being "right."

COMMITMENT 1 day	• guide students through a reflection of new learning and attitude toward spelling. • record student reflection statements for assessment and celebration purposes.	• choose one or two words from their writing that they feel especially proud of and write them on an index card to be displayed. • make a front cover for one of their label books.
TOTAL: 11 DAYS		

Getting Started

Launch this writing unit a week after the reading unit has begun.

Structures and Routines

Partnerships

In the first lessons in this unit, students work in partnerships following the Focused Instruction. Subsequently, students work independently then share their work with partners before coming together at Wrap-Up.

Teaching Materials

Student Materials

Provide different paper choices that enable students to write books with a variety of layouts (see Resources 3.3–3.6).

Play Center Connections

We give students an opportunity to practice spelling strategies and to write labels in their play centers.

Art Center

In this center we make available paper of different shapes and sizes for making signs. Children may create signs for the classroom, another location in the school, or their homes.

Paper Center

Index cards and sticky notes are available for students to write labels for objects in any of the centers.

Stages of the Unit

Immersion

Writing words is introduced through play centers. Students label items throughout the classroom. We show students how to use specific types of paper to label their various play centers and talk about real-world applications for this kind of writing. Students work with a partner to incorporate a label in their play center each day. Writing time starts with Focused Instruction, followed by Independent Practice in the play centers. The Wrap-Up may occur in a central meeting area, or students may travel to one of the centers to study and admire the labeling that was done there.

Identification

Students name the things they do as writers to spell a new word. Chart student responses in this lesson or as you teach each spelling strategy in Guided Practice.

Guided Practice

During this stage, demonstrate spelling strategies that writers use to spell unfamiliar words. Explain that there are two kinds of spelling strategies: sound strategies and sight strategies. Even as proficient adult spellers, we use sound spelling for many words that are unfamiliar to us. So, too, as adults we remember the "look" of words when we are seeking conventional spellings. We recall patterns and combinations that form words we see in the world. Introduce the alphabet chart as a spelling resource for locating the symbol for and/or sound of letters.

During Independent Practice, students write their own label books.

Commitment

We have embedded throughout this unit a positive attitude toward spelling, urging our students not to be afraid of unfamiliar words but rather to forge ahead by choosing a specific spelling strategy. In the Commitment lesson, we ask students to identify spelling strategies that writers use.

Day-by-Day Lessons

DAY 1 Immersion

Focused Instruction

Today we are going to have writing time in our play centers! You will have 15 minutes to play and then I will ask you to stop. You will then work with your partner to identify and label something in your play area.

Independent Practice

- Students use index cards and sticky notes to add labels in their play centers.

Wrap-Up

We will now move from center to center and admire the labels in each area. When we get to your center you will read what you wrote to us.

DAY 2 Immersion

Focused Instruction

We are going to look at how some of you used labels in the housekeeping area.

Independent Practice

We will do the same thing today with our play and writing: you will play for 15 minutes and then you will stop to add a label to your center.

Wrap-Up

We will now move from center to center and admire the labels in each area. When we get to your center, you will read what you wrote to us.

DAY 3 Immersion

Focused Instruction

You have been reading label books during reading time for the past week. Today you will get to write your own label book! You may be wondering what your label book will be about. Often, writers get their ideas from books they have read and enjoyed. Think about the label books you have been reading. What are one or two of your favorites? Think, turn, and tell the person next to you.

Here is a book we all know, Cassie's Word Quilt. *As you know, throughout this story a girl named Cassie talks about her life and where she lives. The author, Faith Ringgold, includes pictures with lots of labels that tell about one part of Cassie's life. You may want to write a label book like* Cassie's Word Quilt. *You could draw a picture that tells a story,*

- Prepare a labeled picture that represents a story you can tell. Show it to the class as an example.

Independent Practice

Today you will choose your paper and begin making your label book.

- Show and explain various paper choices to the students (see Resources 3.3–3.6).

Wrap-Up

You will each get the chance to say the topic of your book and why you chose that topic.

DAY 4 Immersion

Focused Instruction

Many of you have begun making books like Cassie's Word Quilt. *You are making a picture that tells a story and writing labels to name things in your picture. Some of you may be interested in writing nonfiction label books like* My Big Truck Book. *The author of this book knows a lot about trucks, and it seems like he has a big passion for trucks. What are the kinds of things you have passion for that you think you could teach someone about?*

- Show one page of the book and discuss the text layout and information on the page, and how it shows the author's passion for the subject.

Independent Practice

- Students work on label books, either a story or an informational text.
- Differentiating Instruction
  - Strong readers write sentences to accompany the labeled pictures in books. *Snowballs* by Lois Ehlert and *Cassie's Word Quilt* by Faith Ringgold are two examples.

Wrap-Up

Say the topic of your label book and why you chose that topic.

A student writes a label book about things she sees at the pool. Labels on this page read "lifeguard," "whistle," and "chair."

DAY 5 Identification

Focused Instruction

Think for a minute about your own writing. What do you do when you want to write a word that is new for you? Think, turn, and talk to the person next to you. Now let us share with to the rest of the class. Let's read First Word Book *to find new words with which we can practice our spelling.*

- Create a chart from student responses. You may only get one or two strategies from this discussion—that is okay. You will continue to add to this chart as you teach different spelling strategies in the Guided Practice stage.
- Read *First Word Book* to find new words.

Independent Practice

Keep in mind those strategies your classmates have shared for writing new words as you work in your label books today. You can continue a piece of writing from yesterday or begin a new book.

Wrap-Up

Who tried writing a new word in their books today? Maybe it was a word that made you a bit nervous but you said, "I am going to give it a try!" What words are you especially proud of that you spelled in your books today?

DAY 6 Guided Practice

Focused Instruction

I told you that you would learn some strategies that writers use to write words that are unfamiliar to them. One of them is called the sound strategy. Writers say a word slowly and listen to the sounds. They write as many letters as they can for the sounds they hear. Watch me use the sound strategy to write the word "garden."

- For demonstration purposes, you may want to show students how sometimes you are unsure of what letter makes a particular sound so you either make a best guess or put a dash as a placeholder.

Now you will use your dry-erase boards to practice the sound strategy.

- Select a word for all to try.
- Students write as many letters as they can and then turn their boards for you to see. Repeat this process for about three words.
- Do not stop to correct the spelling of the word. At this point we are encouraging students to use this strategy for spelling. We will address conventional spelling later in the year when their visual memory for the way words look begins to develop together with their heightened awareness of English orthography (the ways in which letters and sounds work together).
- Praise students for their efforts.

Independent Practice

As you continue making your label books, try using the sound strategy when you come across an unfamiliar word. Do not worry if there is a long word you want to write in your books. Just use the sound strategy to put as many letters down as you hear.

Wrap-Up

We will go around the circle and you will all share one word you learned today that makes you proud.

DAY 7 Guided Practice

Focused Instruction

You practiced using the sound strategy to spell words yesterday during writing time. Today I am going to show you how to use your alphabet chart (or the classroom alphabet chart) to find the letters you hear when you use the sound strategy.

- Choose words that will be of interest to the students and that apply to the books they are writing.
- Students write and turn their boards to you. Congratulate them for their use of this spelling strategy.

Independent Practice

As you write the words in your books today, use your alphabet chart to find the letters you need to spell new words.

- Differentiating Instruction
  - Provide additional support for vulnerable writers using the alphabet chart as a spelling resource.

Wrap-Up

We will go around the circle and you will each share a word you added to your writing today that makes you proud.

- In addition, you may want to ask three or four students to share the topic of the books they are writing.

DAY 8 Guided Practice

Focused Instruction

Today we are going to look at how information is organized in My Big Truck Book. *This book is about lots of different kinds of trucks. They are organized into categories. There are farm trucks, emergency trucks, big trucks, and so on. So now I am thinking about my garden book and I want to organize information about my garden the same way. I could have a few pages on flowers in my garden, then vegetables, and another section on trees. Some of you may want to try writing a book like this.*

Independent Practice

Try to write some interesting new words in your writing today. Use the sound strategy or your alphabet chart if you need help spelling new words.

Wrap-Up

I am going to share a few topics students wrote about today.

- Discuss book topics that students wrote about earlier and are now revisiting to write more about it or develop it into a larger topic. Example: a page of writing about ballet is developed into a book on a variety of dances; a page of writing on scooters is developed into a book that shows a variety of ride-on toys.

DAY 9 Guided Practice

Focused Instruction

Today I am going to teach you a new spelling strategy called the sight strategy. Sometimes when writers are trying to spell words, they can remember how a familiar word looks in their minds. For example, I want to write the word "toy" and I have seen that word at the store Toys R Us. I am going to close my eyes and try to picture the letters in that word. Now I am going to write the letters I see in my mind. We are all going to use the sight strategy to spell the word "school." Close your eyes and picture the words above the front door of the building—they say "Elementary School." Picture the letters in that last word, "school." Now write the letters that you see in your mind on your board.

- Students write and turn the boards to you. Congratulate them for their use of this spelling strategy.

Independent Practice

As you continue writing words in your label books, try using the sight strategy for an unfamiliar word.

Wrap-Up

- Share some of the topics students are using for their label books. Share words students wrote in their books.

DAY 10 Guided Practice

Focused Instruction

Sometimes you get stuck on a word you want to spell. You may not think you have the correct letter or enough letters. Today we are going to practice saying to ourselves, "Don't worry, keep going." I am going to give you four words to write on your boards today. They are going to be challenging words. Use the spelling strategies you have learned this week to do the best you can and don't worry, keep going!

Independent Practice

Challenge yourself in your writing today to spell words that are interesting and exciting. Do not be afraid to spell words that sound long. Use one of your spelling strategies and don't worry, keep going!

- At the end of Independent Practice, students choose one piece of writing (a book or a labeled picture) that they are most proud of and move it to the front of their folder.

Wrap-Up

Let's go around the room and share one word you wrote in your book today that makes you proud. Say which spelling strategy you used.

DAY 11 Commitment

Focused Instruction

We are going to reflect on what we have learned and celebrate how we have improved as writers over the past two weeks. Which spelling strategy do you find yourself using most often in your writing? Think, turn, and talk to the person next to you. How has your spelling changed during this unit?

- Record student responses.

Independent Practice

Everyone chose a favorite label book from this unit and put it in the front of your folder. Go through that book now and find one word that shows your courage to try spelling new words in new ways to share with others.

- The students write their words on index cards or sentence strips and display them in the room.

I have card stock paper for you to make a front cover for your book. I brought out the special colored pencils to use on your cover.

- Reserve special pencils or markers for publishing a piece of writing. This makes the publishing more exciting and special. Students use them to make a front cover and decorate illustrations inside the books.

Wrap-Up

- Students share their books.

Celebrate and Nurture Oral Language

Deep into winter, the fires of children's energy crackle with a significant attention on collaboration and more-developed partnerships. We want our children to see one another as resources, especially in the kindergarten room where the tug on your sleeve can feel incessant! As much as we adore those little tugs and the smiles that go along with them, it is to our benefit and our students' to create structures that will support their independence and give us the opportunity to confer with individual students. This is why partnership units are so critical at this time of year. Rejuvenating, structured, they send us zooming forward.

By studying the concept of effective partnerships as a unit unto itself, we create time to teach the processes of effective conversation and interaction. Students can try out different ways of helping and supporting one another as readers and writers. Not only is this great for their developing literacy, it also is an opportunity for you to plant seeds in your students about the value of communication. They will see the importance you place on talk and the outcomes from talk: on collaboration, negotiation, support, and engagement.

Deepening Capacity for Talk: Reading Partnerships

PROCESS

Why Teach This?

- To create a reading community in the classroom.
- To build collaboration among readers.
- To teach students the skills necessary to work cooperatively with a peer.

Framing Question

- How do readers read in partnerships?

Unit Goals

- Students will work cooperatively with a partner to read a book.
- Students will take turns reading with a partner.
- Students will sit properly with a book placed between the partners.
- Students will identify and demonstrate the two jobs in a partnership.

Anchor Texts

- *Cross-Country Cat* by Mary Calhoun
- *Where Did You Get Your Moccasins?* by Bernelda Wheeler
- *Harold and the Purple Crayon* by Crockett Johnson

Unit Assessment Deepening Capacity for Talk: Reading Partnerships			PROCESS
Student name:	EMERGING	DEVELOPING	INDEPENDENT
Sits properly with a partner, book placed between them.			
Uses a quiet voice.			
Takes turns reading with a partner.			
Follows along with finger as "the reader" in a partnership.			
Follows along with eyes as "the listener" in a partnership.			
Identifies the jobs of both readers in a partnership.			

Stage of the Unit	Focused Instruction You will	Independent Practice Students will
IMMERSION 1 day	• read *Harold and the Purple Crayon* and model working with a partner (or have two older students come in) to demonstrate the following: sitting side by side, book placed in the middle, one partner following with finger, using a quiet voice.	• practice working with a partner.
IDENTIFICATION 1 day	• read *Cross-Country Cat* and explicitly teach the physicality of working with a partner: sitting side by side, taking turns with fingers on the page, book placed in the middle; point out what partners' bodies are doing during partner reading.	• practice working with a partner, focusing on the physicality of a partnership.
GUIDED PRACTICE 2 days	• model the job of the reader—sitting side by side, following along while reading *Where Did You Get Your Moccasins?* using a quiet voice. • model the job of the listener—sitting side by side, following along with your eyes and not interrupting while the reader reads.	• take turns being the reader in a partnership. • take turns being the listener in a partnership.
COMMITMENT 1 day	• name out three positive behaviors you have noticed in partnerships.	• meet with their partners to celebrate what they can now do together.
TOTAL: 5 DAYS		

Deepening Capacity for Talk: Writing Partnerships

PROCESS

Why Teach This?

- To create a supportive writing community in the classroom.
- To build collaboration.
- To teach students the skills necessary to work cooperatively with a peer.

Framing Question

- How can partnerships help us improve as writers?

Unit Goals

- Students will work cooperatively to share their writing.
- Students will give kind feedback to each other on their writing.

Anchor Texts

- *Ernest and Celestine's Picnic* by Gabrielle Vincent
- *A Splendid Friend Indeed* by Suzanne Bloom

Unit Assessment Deepening Capacity for Talk: Writing Partnerships			PROCESS
Student name:	EMERGING	DEVELOPING	INDEPENDENT
Shares his or her writing with a partner.			
Gives kind feedback to a partner on his or her writing.			

Stage of the Unit	Focused Instruction You will	Independent Practice Students will
IMMERSION 1 day	• use *Ernest and Celestine's Picnic* to discuss how these characters take care of one another. Make a list of how writing partners can take care of one another. • model sharing your own writing with another adult to demonstrate the following: sitting side by side, holding writing, taking turns sharing, and reading aloud together in a supportive manner.	• be assigned a writing partner. Partners will greet one another warmly. • share a piece of writing with their writing partners. This writing can be from a prior unit of study.
IDENTIFICATION 1 day	• name the ways partners look when meeting (body language). • name the purpose for having a writing partner.	• meet with their writing partners before independent practice to share writing ideas. • meet with their writing partners to share completed writing/drawing.

GUIDED PRACTICE 2 days	• model sharing writing ideas with a partner; "I'm going to write a story about…" • model giving kind, specific feedback to a writing partner using the prompt "I wish you would tell me more about…" to identify ways the writer could expand the writing.	• rehearse their writing ideas with partners. • share different pieces of writing and give each other supportive feedback on their writing, using the suggested prompts for compliments ("I like the way you…"; "I wish you would tell me more about…").
COMMITMENT 1 day	• guide students in a reflection of what they now know about working with a partner; record student responses.	• work in partnerships to write and illustrate a letter of appreciation to your partner.
TOTAL: 5 DAYS		

Exploring the World of Genres

Your kindergartener is deeply curious about the world around him. He loves to name things: he loves to know how to do "big kid" things. These next units are designed to introduce the qualities of various genres that he will be seeing and using for the rest of his life. They are the foundation for the work that will come later in the spring season: focused work in genre units that gives him a chance to put on his scientific nonfiction hat, and then his poetry hat. For now, we are exposing him to everything—a buffet of genres! It is a feast.

Exploring the World of Genres: A Reading Unit

GENRE

Why Teach This?

- To expose our youngest readers to the world of genres.
- To introduce our students to the names of different genres.
- To identify simple qualities of genres (poetry, narrative, nonfiction).

Framing Questions

- What different kinds of books do readers read?
- What do we know about different genres?

Unit Goals

- Students will recognize a poem.
- Students will recognize a nonfiction text.
- Students will recognize a storybook or other types of fiction.

Anchor Texts

- *Amazing Grace* by Mary Hoffman
- *Giant Earth Movers (Big Stuff)* by Robert Gould
- *Oil Spill!* by Melvin Berger and Paul Mirocha
- *Sing a Song of Popcorn* selected by Beatrice Schenk de Regniers
- *Tacky the Penguin* by Helen Lester

Unit Assessment Exploring the World of Genres: A Reading Unit			GENRE
Student name:	EMERGING	DEVELOPING	INDEPENDENT
Recognizes a poem.			
Recognizes a nonfiction text.			
Recognizes a storybook (narrative).			

Stage of the Unit	Focused Instruction You will	Independent Practice Students will
IMMERSION 3 days	• read aloud from the poetry anthology *Sing a Song of Popcorn*; notice qualities of poetry (rhythm, fun word sounds). • read aloud from *Tacky the Penguin*; notice qualities of story books (narrative, beginning, middle, end, characters). • read aloud from *Giant Earth Movers*; notice qualities of nonfiction (teaches us something, has photos and visual information, etc.).	• browse in poetry baskets. • browse in story baskets. • browse in nonfiction baskets.
IDENTIFICATION 2 days	• name qualities of poetry, nonfiction, and story. • identify why readers choose one genre over another (create a class chart of these results).	• read with partners the genres they prefer to browse that day.
GUIDED PRACTICE 4 days	• model reading aloud a second poem from *Sing a Song of Popcorn* and identifying elements like the ones we saw in our first set of poems. • model reading aloud *Ricky and Mobo* and noticing elements we saw in our first story, *Tacky the Penguin*. • model reading aloud *Oil Spill!* and noticing elements we see.	• read/browse using sticky notes to highlight elements of poetry. • read/browse, using sticky notes to highlight elements of story. • read/browse, using sticky notes to highlight elements of nonfiction.
COMMITMENT 2 days	• reflect on two things we have noticed about each kind of genre.	• help organize the classroom library with baskets of books organized by genre.
TOTAL: 11 DAYS		

Exploring the World of Genres: A Writing Unit

GENRE

Why Teach This?

- To expose our writers to the world of genres.
- To introduce our writers to the names of different genres.
- To identify simple qualities of genres (poetry, narrative, nonfiction).

Framing Question

- What different genres do writers write?

Unit Goals

- Students will recognize a poem.
- Students will recognize a narrative.
- Students will recognize nonfiction.

Anchor Texts

- *Giant Earth Movers (Big Stuff)* by Robert Gould
- *Sing a Song of Popcorn* selected by Beatrice Schenk de Regniers
- *Tacky the Penguin* by Helen Lester

Unit Assessment Exploring the World of Genres: A Writing Unit			GENRE
Student name:	EMERGING	DEVELOPING	INDEPENDENT
Writes or draws a poem.			
Writes or draws a nonfiction information booklet.			
Writes or draws a storybook (narrative).			

Stage of the Unit	Focused Instruction You will	Independent Practice Students will
IMMERSION 3 days	• read aloud from the poetry anthology *Sing a Song of Popcorn*. Notice qualities of poetry (rhythm, fun word sounds). • read aloud from *Tacky the Penguin* by Helen Lester; notice qualities of storybooks (narrative): beginning, middle, end, characters. • read aloud from *Where Does the Mail Go?*; notice qualities of nonfiction (teaches us something, has photos and visual information).	• browse in poetry baskets. • browse in story baskets. • browse in nonfiction baskets.
IDENTIFICATION 2 days	• name qualities of poetry, nonfiction, and story. • identify why readers choose one genre over another (create a classroom chart with this information).	• read with partners based on the genre they prefer to read or browse that day.
GUIDED PRACTICE 4 days	• model writing a poem and identifying elements like the ones we saw in our first set of poems. • model writing a narrative based on what we noticed in *Tacky the Penguin.* • model writing a nonfiction piece based on what we noticed in *Giant Earth Movers*	• brainstorm writing ideas through the four prompts (wonder, remember, imagine, observe). • try writing one idea as a poem. • try writing the same idea as a narrative. • try writing the same idea as nonfiction.
COMMITMENT 2 days	• reflect on things we have noticed about each kind of genre.	• share their writing in a "genres museum"; students dictate a description of the genre in which they wrote; that description is displayed along with corresponding student writing— similar to a museum exhibit!
TOTAL: 11 DAYS		

Choice: An Important Component in the Lives of Readers and Writers

This set of units is integral to the entire year. See them as a bridge between the first part of the year and the second. In the first part of the year, you are setting the stage for your writers by introducing the routines and habits of effective readers and writers, setting the foundations for story and for making meaning from story. Now, you are turning a corner: bringing your students toward a new kind of independence and self-sufficiency as readers and writers. In the second half of the year, we will explore genres of poetry, fiction, and nonfiction together, requiring a greater capacity for independence and idea building. Your students need an infusion of support on choices: how readers make them and how writers make them, scaffolding their independence as they enter new worlds.

Making Choices as Readers   PROCESS

Why Teach This?
- To empower students to select and read texts that interest them and are at their level.
- To teach students how readers identify their reading preferences.
- To help students share their reading passions and interests with their peers.

Framing Question
- How do readers choose books they like to read?

Unit Goals
- Students will choose and read books within a self-selected topic or genre.
- Students will read books on a variety of topics and within a variety of genres to find their "picks."
- Students will share their reading passions with a partner.

Anchor Texts
- *Look Out for Turtles* by Melvin Berger
- *My Father's Hands* by Joanne Ryder
- *The Sun Is So Quiet* by Nikki Giovanni
- *Tell Me a Story, Mama* by Angela Johnson

Unit Assessment Making Choices as Readers			PROCESS
Student name:	EMERGING	DEVELOPING	INDEPENDENT
Reads books that vary in topic, genre, and author.			
Uses book covers to inform book choices in the library.			
Chooses books within a self-selected topic or genre.			
Reads books within a self-selected topic or genre.			
Explains book choices.			
Shares reading picks with a partner.			

Stage of the Unit	Focused Instruction You will	Independent Practice Students will
IMMERSION 2 days	• bring in a selection of favorite books (they may be dog-eared and aged); briefly share what makes them your favorite picks. • share one specific, meaningful pick.	• draw a picture of their favorite book. • share their pictures with a partner and describe why the book is a favorite.
IDENTIFICATION 3 days	• use *Look Out for Turtles* to model browsing in the library. • explore the library, thinking aloud, going through bins and using the covers to guide your choices.	• explore the library using their favorite book as a guide to finding new books. • explore specific genre bins.
GUIDED PRACTICE 4 days	• choose a poem from *The Sun Is So Quiet* to look at genre, author, character, and series, and read within the genre for one of two days; think aloud about what you like about a particular poem—What do readers talk about when they describe their pick? • introduce phrases readers can use to share their picks with a partner ("I like this because…"; "I chose this book because…"); read *Tell Me a Story, Mama* and model sharing a book with a partner.	• choose one kind of book to focus on and read within that category for one or two days. • specifically identify what they like about a pick, then share with a partner. • share their picks with a partner using specific phrases to guide the conversation.
COMMITMENT 1 day	• create a picture for *My Father's Hands* and write why you would recommend this book; these "book pick" posters can hang in the library.	• create a "book pick" picture and write a recommendation of the book to another reader.
TOTAL: 10 DAYS		

Making Choices as Writers: The Four Prompts

Why Teach This?
- To empower students to choose what they want to write.
- To teach students how to generate writing ideas.
- To teach students how writers go back and add on to their writing pieces.

Framing Question
- How do writers find writing ideas?

Unit Goals
- Students will identify ways that writers get ideas.
- Students will use the Four Prompts to generate writing ideas.
- Students will choose one writing idea to expand on.
- Students will add more details to a piece of writing they've selected.

Anchor Texts
- *Look Out for Turtles* by Melvin Berger
- *My Father's Hands* by Joanne Ryder
- *Some Dogs Do* by Jez Alborough
- *The Sun Is So Quiet* by Nikki Giovanni
- *Tell Me a Story, Mama* by Angela Johnson

Unit Assessment Making Choices as Writers: The Four Prompts			PROCESS
Student name:	EMERGING	DEVELOPING	INDEPENDENT
Remembers one way he or she came up with a writing idea this year.			
Makes a list or draws pictures of writing ideas using the prompt "I wonder…"			
Makes a list or draws pictures of writing ideas using the prompt "I imagine…"			
Makes a list or draws pictures of writing ideas using the prompt "I observe…"			
Makes a list or draws pictures of writing ideas using the prompt "I remember…"			
Expands writing on one topic from a list or a picture.			
Adds details to a self-selected idea or piece of writing.			

Stage of the Unit	Focused Instruction You will	Independent Practice Students will
IMMERSION 1 day	• share favorite read-aloud books for the year; think aloud about how the writers may have gotten the ideas for those books.	• choose one favorite book and think about how the writer came up with the idea for the book; share their idea with their partners.
IDENTIFICATION 1 day	• think aloud about your work as a writer this year, remembering ways you came up with ideas for your writing; read aloud from *The Sun Is So Quiet* and make a class chart to list where Nikki Giovanni got her ideas.	• identify one idea they found for a story this year and where it came from; share where their idea came from and list them on the class chart.
GUIDED PRACTICE 7 days	• introduce the Four Prompts chart and explain how writers use them to think of ideas (I wonder, I remember, I observe, I imagine). • read aloud *Look Out for Turtles* and model making a list and drawing pictures of writing ideas from the prompt "I wonder…" • read aloud from *Some Dogs Do* and model using the prompt "I imagine…" to create a list and drawings of writing ideas. • read *My Father's Hands* and model using the prompt "I observe…" to create a list and drawings of writing ideas. • read *Tell Me a Story, Mama* and model using the prompt "I remember…" to create a list and drawings of writing ideas. • choose one idea from one of your lists or pictures that you want to write more about and demonstrate how you would add to your thinking.	• create lists and pictures of things they could write about using the prompt "I wonder…" • create lists and pictures of things they could write about using the prompt "I imagine…" • create lists and pictures of things they could write about using the prompt "I observe…" • create lists and pictures of things they could write about using the prompt "I remember…" • choose an idea from one of their lists or pictures to write more about during Independent Practice.
COMMITMENT 1 day	• model going back to one writing piece inspired by a prompt and choose that one to publish; model adding on to your writing with more detail, then share that piece with a partner when you are finished.	• choose one of their writing pieces that they want to publish; add on to their writing with more detail, then share their writing with a partner.
TOTAL: 10 DAYS		

From Late Fall to Winter

Your kindergartener has been exploring worlds of genre, worlds of talk, worlds of language. Now as the winter deepens, your students are able to read and write with greater stamina, and so you will teach the skills and strategies they must develop to truly thrive in their literacy development for longer periods of time. Poetry fills the air, and we use the beats and rhythms of language to propel our children into the world of fluency.

Chapter 4

WINTER

The Kindergartener as Strategic Reader and Writer

"I want to be old but not so old that Mars and Jupiter and redwoods seem young. I want to be fast but not so fast that lightning seems slow. I want to be wise but not so wise that I can't learn anything."

—from *I Want to Be* by Thylias Moss

Kindergarteners are like sponges. They can absorb, learn, and grow all in the space of one day. They are capable of so much, and if presented wisely and well, the material does not overwhelm them. Rather, your teaching gives them the tools they need to become truly strategic as readers and writers from the youngest age. Take a journey with us into this next set of winter units of study in reading and writing.

WINTER UNITS

SPOTLIGHT
UNITS

Strengthening Muscles for Reading and Writing

It is fascinating and wonderful to watch the imaginative play of kindergarteners on the playground, alone or with peers. Midyear, they can sustain ideas over time—build a fort and come back to it the next day, make a game that goes on and on. Their stamina is high for play, and one idea builds on another and another. We can learn a great deal from them in how they stick with an idea and how they use one another's ideas to construct new ones. Our goal is to create this same energy in their reading and writing experiences. The word "stamina" is not meant to imply that we should force our kindergarteners to read and write longer, longer, longer until they are exhausted! Instead, we can develop their stamina during this time of year by celebrating and reinforcing their capacity to stick with ideas and return to them, and to linger with books for longer periods of time.

Building Stamina: Reading Long and Strong

PROCESS

Why Teach This?

- To teach reading behaviors and strategies that help develop reading stamina.
- To build students' reading stamina.

Framing Questions

- How do effective readers read long and strong?

Unit Goals

- Students will identify behaviors that build reading stamina.
- Students will understand various purposes for rereading a favorite book.
- Students will read for longer periods of time.

Anchor Texts

- *Alice, the Fairy* by David Shannon
- *Bear Snores On* by Karma Wilson
- *A Box Full of Kittens* by Sonia Manzano
- *Shy Charles* by Rosemary Wells
- *Strega Nona* by Tomie dePaola

Unit Assessment Building Stamina: Reading Long and Strong			PROCESS
Student name:	EMERGING	DEVELOPING	INDEPENDENT
Makes decisions about reading conditions that increase stamina.			
Increases reading stamina by rereading a favorite book.			
Reads for extended periods of time.			

Stage of the Unit	Focused Instruction You will	Independent Practice Students will
IMMERSION 3 days	• show a video of a first-grade class (or visit one) during their independent reading time; discuss what we can observe about these readers. • reflect on what makes you comfortable when you read. • reflect on how you know when you feel strong as a reader and when you do not.	• investigate reading behaviors of readers who can read for long periods of time and feel strong as readers. • notice their own reading behaviors during independent practice: Are they feeling strong? Can they read comfortably until the end of independent reading time? • reflect on the times when they did and did not feel strong in their reading.
IDENTIFICATION 1 day	• use *A Box Full of Kittens* to identify and chart the things readers can do to read longer and stronger: they read books that are interesting, they do not rush through their books but "linger" inside them; they read in a spot that is comfortable and where they will not be distracted.	• practice behaviors and skills listed on the chart in order to read longer and stronger.
GUIDED PRACTICE 6 days	• use *Bear Snores On* to discuss and chart how we can linger with our books by rereading; discuss various purposes for rereading. • use *Shy Charles* to discuss how you can tell the story through the pictures. • use *Strega Nona* to model for students how to use character voices when reading or telling the story. • use *Alice, the Fairy* to model how to read the words smoothly, and how to notice more in the picture or photograph. • revisit an anchor text to show how rereading helps a reader to read long and strong. • demonstrate revisiting a favorite part of a book and thinking about why it is a favorite.	• read, then reread one of their books practicing what was demonstrated in the focused instruction. • tell a story through the pictures. • use characters' voices when reading or telling the story. • read words smoothly or notice details in the pictures. • think about why a specific part is a favorite. • mark a favorite part in a book and discuss with partners the page and why it is their favorite.
COMMITMENT 1 day	• identify what you now notice about the stamina of your students; ask students to make a list of eight to ten things you can teach someone about how to read longer and stronger.	• list five things that kindergarteners can do to read longer and stronger; work in small groups to illustrate pages in a class big book called *Five Ways to Read Longer and Stronger!*
TOTAL: 11 DAYS		

Building Stamina: Writing Long and Strong

PROCESS

Why Teach This?

- To teach behaviors and strategies that will help develop writing stamina.
- To build students' writing stamina.

Framing Question

- How do writers write long and strong?

Unit Goals

- Students will identify behaviors and strategies that build writing stamina.
- Students will write for longer periods of time.

Anchor Texts

- *My Father's Hands* by Joanne Ryder
- *Please, Baby, Please* by Spike Lee and Tanya Lewis Lee

Unit Assessment Building Stamina: Writing Long and Strong			PROCESS
Student name:	EMERGING	DEVELOPING	INDEPENDENT
Chooses writing topics of importance.			
Writes about a beloved topic in various genres as a way to extend stamina.			
Plans writing through talk and drawings.			
Rereads writing to add new details.			

Stage of the Unit	Focused Instruction You will	Independent Practice Students will
IMMERSION 2 days	• tell about a time when you could write long and strong; reflect on what contributed to the increased stamina (writing spot, the genre, the topic, the audience). • demonstrate for students how you continue writing (using spelling strategies, for example) when writing feels hard.	• spy on another class during independent writing and discuss what they notice. • reflect on times when they felt strong or did not feel strong as writers.

IDENTIFICATION 1 day	• identify and chart behaviors that help writers write long and strong: writing about topics they care about (show the book *Please, Baby, Please* as an example of someone writing about a topic that matters), writing about a beloved topic in different genres, figuring out what they will write by talking and planning with a partner, using spelling strategies to get through the hard parts.	• practice behaviors of writers who write long and strong.
GUIDED PRACTICE 6 days	• use *My Father's Hands* to discuss how writers choose their topics (ask, "Where do writers get their ideas? Is my topic interesting to me? Do I have a lot to say about my topic?"). • model writing about one topic in various genres (a story about when I got my dog, a nonfiction book about dogs, a letter to my grandmother telling her about how great my dog is, a poem about dogs). • model how writers make plans for writing by talking with a partner before writing. • model the technique of telling a story across the pages and sketching your ideas to help you remember your writing plans (tell the story aloud as you turn the pages of the booklet, decide what goes on each page; make a quick sketch of what will go on each page). • discuss what to do if you feel done with your writing but independent writing time is not over: add more to the drawings or words, start a new piece of writing, revisit an old piece of writing and add more.	• choose a topic about which they have a lot to say. • write about a beloved topic in various genres. • think about their topic and plan their writing by talking about it with a partner. • practice telling their story across the pages and sketching their ideas. • practice using new strategies to help continue writing for longer periods of time (comfortably!).
COMMITMENT 1 day	• reflect on what you now notice about the writing stamina of the students; ask students to list five things writers can do to write long and strong; write their ideas on chart paper, to be turned into a big book.	• share five things that writers can do to write long and strong; work in small groups to illustrate pages in a class big book called *Five Ways to Write Longer and Stronger!*
TOTAL: 10 DAYS		

SPOTLIGHT on Strategy

- Retelling Using Story Elements
- Revisiting a Favorite Text to Inspire Writing

Strategy is thinking about what tools (physical or cognitive) we need and have available to understand and solve a problem, create a plan, and put the plan into action to solve the problem. The effective reader and writer and thinker asks: What are the ways of looking at this problem others have successfully employed, and what are the "tricks of the trade" I can use? We often spend time teaching different strategies separately (making connections or asking questions, for example) when the real challenge is to help our children understand what type of strategy would be best used to solve a particular problem, and then to identify the particular strategy to solve it. The strategies we use as readers and writers depend on our intuitive understanding of what is happening in that moment as we read and write, and how that relates to the goal we are trying to achieve. By properly identifying the problem, we can use the right strategy to fix it.

In *An Observational Survey of Early Literacy Achievement*, Marie Clay (2003) noted that children under the age of eight who are learning new or complex information thrive with teachers who observe how students solve problems and then use that knowledge to create differentiated instruction.

Strategy units are about helping our students to build these powers of concentration, "planfulness," connections, and inquiry as they explore new or complex information in their literacy journeys. Retelling is a powerful reading strategy for comprehension; looking closely at one text is a powerful strategy writers use to plan their writing. We will take a close look at both. For more information on strategy units possibilities in kindergarten and how we can categorize strategies to teach them effectively, please see pages 73 to 79 of my book *The Complete 4 for Literacy*.

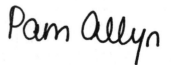

The World of Story

The kindergartener loves to retell stories: her story, her friend's story, an author's story! Retelling is a natural strategy for developing comprehension, and research has shown us that the more children can do it, the earlier they read and the stronger their reading skills are. Retelling is like rehearsal: it is a muscle game for the brain, but it is not just a game, it is a lifelong skill.

Retelling Using Story Elements

STRATEGY

Why Teach This?

- To give students an understanding of the purposes for retelling.
- To make the connection between retelling and students' prior learning about story elements.
- To teach students how to retell effectively.

Framing Question

- Why do readers retell books?
- What makes up a strong retelling?

Unit Goals

- Students will understand the purposes for retelling.
- Students will retell main story elements.
- Students will retell plot events sequentially and accurately.
- Students will retell using a conversational tone.
- Students will state their opinion of a book in their retelling.
- Students will collaborate with partners to retell.

Anchor Texts

- *Caps for Sale* by Esphyr Slobodkina
- *For You Are a Kenyan Child* by Kelly Cunnane
- *The Road to Mumbai* by Ruth Jeyaveeran
- *Sylvester and the Magic Pebble* by William Steig
- *Tacky the Penguin* by Helen Lester
- *Wemberly Worried* by Kevin Henkes

Resource Sheet

- Parent Letter (Resource 4.1)

Unit Assessment Retelling Using Story Elements			STRATEGY
Student name:	EMERGING	DEVELOPING	INDEPENDENT
Identifies past retelling experiences.			
Understands the purpose for retelling stories.			
Includes key story ingredients (story elements) in retelling.			
Retells using a conversational tone.			
Retells the title of a book.			
Includes main character(s) in retelling.			
Includes a statement about time or place in retelling.			
Retells the problem and solution.			
Retells story sequentially and accurately.			

Stage of the Unit	Focused Instruction You will	Independent Practice Students will
IMMERSION 3 days	• discuss the meaning of and purposes for retelling. • reflect on favorite books you want to retell to others. • model retelling a familiar and a new book. • demonstrate retelling the title of a book.	• retell events from their lives. • look through past read-aloud books and choose their favorites for retelling. • try retelling past read-alouds.
IDENTIFICATION 3 days	• name the parts of a story to include in a retelling (Story Ingredients). • help students name the qualities of a strong retelling.	• include the story ingredients in their retellings. • retell books with an attention to the qualities that make the retelling strong.
GUIDED PRACTICE 9 days	• use *Caps for Sale* to demonstrate taking a picture walk to remind yourself of how a story goes. • model retelling *Caps for Sale* using a conversational tone. • demonstrate retelling the main characters in *The Road to Mumbai*. • demonstrate how readers must sometimes infer the setting of stories. • model identifying then retelling the problem in a story. • model identifying then retelling the solution to a story's problem.	• take a picture walk (if necessary) to refresh their memory of books before retelling. • retell a story to stuffed animals using a conversational tone. • include just the main characters in their retellings. • identify and include the setting of stories in their retellings. • identify and retell the problem in a story. • mark the problem and solution in a story with sticky notes; include in retelling.

GUIDED PRACTICE *(continued)*	• model using a Story String to organize and sequence retelling.	• use Story Strings to organize and sequence retelling.
GUIDED PRACTICE *(continued)*	• model how readers state their opinion of a book before retelling; create a classroom chart of possible opinions. • model imagining an ideal audience for retelling.	• state their opinion of a book before retelling. • draw their ideal audience and retell to their picture.
COMMITMENT 1 day	• guide students through a reflection on what they've learned during this unit.	• orally reflect on how they have improved as readers. • retell a favorite book to an audience of a stuffed animal and a friend. • draw a picture of their favorite book, one they want to continue retelling to others.
TOTAL: 16 DAYS		

Structures and Routines

Partnerships
Most of the retellings students do in this unit are from past read-alouds. Because the class is familiar with these texts, students can support each other's retellings in authentic and purposeful ways. When forming partnerships in this unit, consider pairing students who have similar book interests.

Teaching Materials
The best choices for anchor texts are those stories that have good picture support, a strong narrative thread, and a clear sequence of events.

Choosing the Texts for Students to Read
These books are organized in table top baskets for two to three partnerships to share.

- *Ananzi the Spider: A Tale From the Ashanti* by Gerald McDermott
- *Baby, Come Out!* by Fran Manushkin
- *Bear Snores On* by Karma Wilson
- *Caps for Sale* by Esphyr Slobodkina
- *Corduroy* by Don Freeman
- *The Fourth Little Pig* by Teresa Celsi
- *Fredrick* by Leo Lionni
- *Froggy Goes to School* by Jonathan London
- *I Will Never Not Eat a Tomato* by Lauren Child
- *Jim and the Beanstalk* by Raymond Briggs

- *Kitten's First Full Moon* by Kevin Henkes
- *Koala Lou* by Mem Fox
- *Lost and Found* by Oliver Jeffers
- *The Mitten* by Jan Brett
- *The Paper Bag Princess* by Robert Munsch
- *Pete's a Pizza* by William Steig
- *Ruby the Copy Cat* by Peggy Rathmann
- *Sheila Rae the Brave* by Kevin Henkes
- *Somebody and the Three Blairs* by Marilyn Tolhurst
- *Strega Nona* by Tomie dePaola
- *Superhero* by Marc Tauss
- *Swimmy* by Leo Lionni
- *Tacky the Penguin* by Helen Lester
- *Tikki Tikki Tembo* by Blair Lent
- *The True Story of the Three Little Pigs* by Jon Scieszka
- *Wemberly Worried* by Kevin Henkes

Differentiation

Some of your students may be reading fluently and therefore able to retell the books they are reading independently. Below are some narratives for beginning readers.

A Bug, a Bear, and a Boy series by David McPhail:

- *Play Hide-and-Seek*
- *Plant a Garden*
- *And the Bath*
- *At Home*

Student Materials

Story Strings

The Story Strings used in the early fall for oral storytelling are used again in this unit. The icons representing the various story elements remain the same but retelling events becomes more sophisticated in this unit.

There are two icons on the string that represent important events in the plot, followed by a bow, which is the "tie-up," or ending to the story. We explain that many books present a problem in the beginning of the story. We teach students to include the problem as the first event in their retelling and the solution to the problem at the "tie-up" on the string.

Stuffed Animals

Students will practice retelling a book in a conversational tone using a cozy stuffed animal as a prop.

A Story String is used to aide students in their retelling of familiar books.

Play Center Connections

Retelling stories is a natural fit for many of your play centers. At this time of the year, retelling breathes new life into the regularity of centers.

Block Area

A tabletop basket is placed in the block or Lego area. We demonstrate for the students how to build the setting of a story and retell that part of the story to a friend. Students can also build the setting of a story and then ask others to guess the story. Often we have signs, people, and cars available in the block area; those can be used to add details to the structure. Students may want to add labels in order to include even more information about the setting.

Art Center

Students make paintings or drawings of their favorite characters from past read-alouds. These are posted on a bulletin board titled "Our Favorite Book Characters."

Dramatic Play

Provide props that allow children the ability to act out a favorite story. Some examples:

- *The Paper Bag Princess*: a paper bag (holes cut for head and arms), a crown, a dragon puppet, a male doll
- *Superhero*: a cape, plants and/or flowers (real or artificial)

Computer Center

A basket of Story Strings and favorite books are put in an area where children can record themselves, either with a tape recorder or a computer. Students choose a favorite book and practice retelling it to a partner using a conversational tone. This center is introduced after Day 12 of the unit, when the tone of a retelling is taught. Children continue to use this center even as the reading instruction goes into a new unit of study.

Stages of the Unit

Immersion

We start by asking students to identify retelling experiences that occur naturally in the course of a day. We ask students to think back to favorite books they have heard this year and collect them in tabletop baskets. Students use these books to take picture walks with a partner, reviewing key points in the stories. A parent letter can be sent home at this time (see Resources 4.1).

Identification

We go back to prior learning once again in this stage. Here we ask students to recall what they know about story elements by identifying the story ingredients we studied in the fall. During

Independent Practice, partnerships identify the various story elements in their books. We introduce the idea that stories often have a problem presented in the beginning of the book. When identifying three plot events (as was learned previously), students should include the problem and the solution.

Guided Practice

During the Focused Instruction, one aspect of a strong retelling is modeled each day. Students then work in their partnerships to practice with a book from their tabletop basket. The students' retellings will become longer and more detailed each day. Some students may love a particular book and want to stick with it for a number of days, retelling more and more of the story each day. Others may want to retell a different story each day. When students are asked to retell the problem in their stories, we use Story Strings.

Using specific story elements to retell helps students to include important information and retell sequentially. At the same time, retellings can sound robotic. In this stage, we model retelling using a conversational tone. Students talk about their ideal audience and imagine that audience during their retelling to improve the tone of their delivery.

Commitment

On the last day of the unit, students reflect on what they have learned and identify the qualities of a strong retelling. We want the students to see how this reading skill can be useful in their lives and identify an audience and purpose for retelling stories outside of school.

Day-by-Day Lessons

DAY 1 Immersion

Focused Instruction

We retell because we love a story and want to think about it again. We retell to remind us of the details of something we care about. We retell to let someone else know what happened.

- Retell an event for students.

Independent Practice

Think of something that happened that you want to tell your partner about. Tell a story to your partner.

Wrap-Up

Let's revisit all the reasons people retell. Give me a thumbs-up when I say one of the reasons if it is why you chose your story to tell today.

DAY 2 Immersion

Focused Instruction

Retelling means to tell something again. The stories you retold to one another were of events that stood out in your minds—mostly things that have happened that you enjoyed. Today I want you to think about the stories I have read to you that you really enjoyed. Each of us has a number of books that we love, books we could hear over and over. They are the books we go home and tell our parents about. Sylvester and the Magic Pebble *is one of those books for me. I am going to retell it to you now. Pay attention to the parts of the book I choose to include in my retelling.*

- Retell a familiar book.

Independent Practice

I have put a number of past read-alouds at each group's table. Choose one of the books and try retelling it with your partner.

Wrap-Up

What are some of your favorite books from this year—the books you want to tell others about?

- Make a list of favorite read-alouds. Add these books into the tabletop baskets for the remainder of this unit.

DAY 3 Immersion

Focused Instruction

I read a new book yesterday that I just loved! Let me tell you about it. The book is called For You Are a Kenyan Child *by Kelly Cunnane.*

- Retell this book to the class.

Independent Practice

I have placed some of your favorite books in your tabletop baskets. I would like you to work with your partner, choose one of the books in the basket, and retell it together. You can use the pictures in the book to remind yourself of the story.

Wrap-Up

Let's go over the story ingredients that are on our Story String.

- Review the elements represented by various icons.

How might our Story String help us to retell books?

DAY 4 Identification

Focused Instruction

Our Story Strings can help us to give a strong and clear retelling of a book, just like they helped us with our storytelling. Let's name the parts of a story we will include in a retelling.

- Revisit story ingredients chart from the fall storytelling unit or create a new one with the following information:

Person/animal = who is in the story (characters)	
House/tree = where and when the story is taking place (setting)	
Two buttons = two important events that happened in the story	
Bow = how the story ties up, or ends	

- Sketch an image of the icons on your Story String onto the chart.

I will retell one of our favorite books, Tacky the Penguin.
I need to start my retelling by saying the title of the book. Give me a thumbs-up when you hear me talk about one of our story ingredients.

Independent Practice

Each partnership will get a Story String to use today. Choose a book from the tabletop basket and use the string as a reminder of what to include in your retelling. Remember to start with the title of the book.

Wrap-Up

Let's use a Story String to retell Wemberly Worried *by Kevin Henkes.*

- Using a Story String, choose a familiar book to retell together, start with the title.

A teacher uses an extra-large Story String in her Focused Instruction.

DAY 5 Identification

Focused Instruction

To do a strong retell, you need to remember a story well. Doing a picture walk before retelling a story will remind you of how the story goes and the ingredients you want to mix into your retelling.

- Model this with an enlarged text, such as *Caps for Sale*.

Independent Practice

Before you begin retelling a book today, take a picture walk with your partner. Remind each other of what happened in the story. Then go back and retell, making sure you mix in all the ingredients you need to get a strong and clear retelling.

- Differentiating Instruction
    - Strong readers read a book independently, then retell it to a partner.

Wrap-Up

Listen to me as I retell the beginning of Caps for Sale.

- Speak with little expression.

Now listen to me tell it again.

- Use a storytelling tone.

Which retelling is stronger? Which one would you rather listen to and why?

DAY 6 Identification

Focused Instruction

We are learning about retelling books. What do you know about strong retellings? Let's name the qualities of a strong retelling.

- Chart the qualities of a strong retelling.

A strong retelling:
• includes the story ingredients in a book.
• includes the title of the book.
• sounds like you are talking.

Independent Practice

Work with a partner to choose a book from your basket to retell today. Remember what we said about the qualities of a strong retelling. Try to include those things in your retelling today.

Wrap-Up

- Choose a pair of students to share the retelling they did during Independent Practice time.

What makes this retelling strong?

DAY 7 Guided Practice

Focused Instruction

We want our retellings to sound like we are having a conversation. I have a basket of stuffed animals with me. You are going to choose one and bring it to your reading spot. Cuddle with your animal. Tell it all about your book. Remember to mix in the ingredients you need for a clear and strong retelling.

Independent Practice

- Students read and retell with their stuffed animals.

Wrap-Up

- Have two students share a retelling.

Students retell to their stuffed animals using a conversational tone.

DAY 8 Guided Practice

Focused Instruction

Characters are the people or animals the story is about. Some stories have lots of characters in them, like The Road to Mumbai. *Some characters are more important than others. When I retell a book, I tell the characters the book is mostly about.*

Independent Practice

Choose a book to retell with your partner. Take a picture walk first if you feel you need to remember what the story is about. Talk about who the main characters are in the story— who the book is mostly about. When you retell, be sure to say those characters' names.

Wrap-Up

Here is one of the tabletop baskets. I am going to hold up a few of the books that we know well. Let us say who the main characters are in each story.

DAY 9 Guided Practice

Focused Instruction

Some authors tell the reader where the story is taking place. When we read the beginning of For You Are a Kenyan Child, *"Roosters crow and you wake up in the green hills of Africa," we know right away the setting for this story is Africa. Some stories do not say where the action is taking place. Readers have to figure it out from looking at the pictures. I am going to show you the pictures in* Sylvester and the Magic Pebble, *and I want you to think about the setting—the where and when of the story.*

- Ask students to share the clues about setting they found in a book.

Independent Practice

With your partner, talk about where the story you are retelling takes place. If the time of year or time of day is important to the story, talk about that, too. When you retell the story, make sure you mix in the setting.

Wrap-Up

I have a few books from the tabletop baskets. Let's talk about the setting for these books.

DAY 10 Guided Practice

Focused Instruction

In many of the stories you have been retelling, there is a problem that the character tries to fix or solve. In Sylvester and the Magic Pebble, *Sylvester turns into a rock. In* For You Are a Kenyan Child, *the boy loses his herd. When there is a problem in a story, that is an important part to retell. These two books come from the book baskets. Let's retell the problem in these stories.*

Independent Practice

Choose one book from the basket. If it is new to you, take a picture walk first. Talk about the story and whether there is a problem in it. Retell the story and be sure to include the problem if there is one.

Wrap-Up

- Choose a partnership to model a retelling for the class.

DAY 11 Guided Practice

Focused Instruction

When there is a problem in a story, the ending of the book usually tells us how the problem is solved. When you get to the tie-up on your Story String, tell how the problem was solved. Watch me as I retell one of the books from the basket. Listen to me retell the problem and then how the problem was solved at the end.

- Retell a familiar story.

A strong retelling includes how a problem is solved.

Independent Practice

Today you and your partner will get two sticky notes. One note will go on the page where you found a problem in your story. You will write a "P" on that note. The second one will go where the problem is solved. You will put an "S" on that note. Practice retelling the story one at a time to your partner. Use your Story String to remind yourself of all you need to mix in to make a strong and clear retelling.

Wrap-Up

- Ask two partnerships to retell the problem and then the solution in their books to the class.

DAY 12 Guided Practice

Focused Instruction

Today you will practice giving a strong and clear retelling to a stuffed animal. Before Independent Practice, we are going to retell this book together. Let's use the Story String to remind ourselves of the parts to mix in.

- Choose a familiar story for the class to retell together.

Independent Practice

Choose a stuffed animal and retell a book to it. Remember to sound like you are having a conversation.

Wrap-Up

Meet with your kindergarten partner and retell your book to him or her.

DAY 13 Guided Practice

Focused Instruction

When I want to tell someone about a book, I start by saying the title and why I like the book. I might say, "I read this book, Tacky the Penguin. *I like it because it is so funny!" or "*For You Are a Kenyan Child *is a book I just read. I love it because it is so beautifully written." I am going to hold up some of our books and we are going to give our opinion of the book—how we feel about it. We are going to use the word "because" to explain our thinking.*

- You may want to chart the various opinions with sketches.

Independent Practice

- Partners retell stories to each other.

Wrap-Up

Strong retellings begin with the reader's opinion of the book.

DAY 14 Guided Practice

Focused Instruction

Let's review all we have learned about strong retellings.

- Ask a partnership or an individual student to give a retelling of a favorite book.

Independent Practice

Today you will retell your book to a stuffed animal. Remember to start with the title and your opinion of the book.

Wrap-Up

- Name specific qualities of a strong retelling that students incorporated.

DAY 15 Guided Practice

Focused Instruction

Readers retell with an audience in mind. Today, I am going to draw you my favorite audience for my own retellings (you, the children!). When I imagine my favorite audience, I feel comfortable and my retellings sound like a conversation. Today, during Independent Practice, I want you to draw your ideal audience: it can be an imaginary friend, your pet at home, your friends in school, your grandma, and so on. Then we are going to tape our picture of our ideal audience to a chair or our desk so we can practice retelling to our audience.

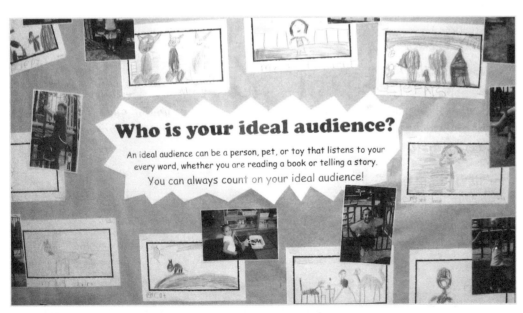

A bulletin board shows students' ideal audiences. Imagining this audience while retelling helps students to feel comfortable and use a conversational tone.

my art Innat

my dog kiiro

Examples of kindergarteners' ideal audiences.

Independent Practice

Draw your ideal audience and place the picture where you can see it.

Wrap-Up

Share your ideal audience with a partner.

DAY 16 Commitment

Focused Instruction

We are going to have a retelling celebration today. Retelling favorite stories is something we should all continue to do even though we are ending this unit of study. Think about one person whom you will continue to retell books to—perhaps it is your ideal audience. Tell the person next to you who your audience will be.

Independent Practice

Now we are going to show off our retelling skills to one another. Choose a stuffed animal, a favorite book, and classmate (it does not have to be your partner). Go to an area of the room and take turns retelling your books.

Wrap-Up

• The celebration continues.

You will draw a picture of your favorite book, one that you would like to retell to friends.

Admiration and Emulation

Great writers have books on their desks and favorite lines taped to their computer monitors. We can help our students find mentors in writing and use them to polish their own. The young child watches his mother bake a cake. She stirs the eggs briskly with a fork; she eyes the measuring cup and pours the flour carefully. When he plays in the kitchen, he does the same thing. He stirs in his pretend bowl, he eyes his measuring cup. They are watching us all the time! Let us give them many mentors to watch and emulate. In writing, too.

Revisiting a Favorite Text to Inspire Writing

STRATEGY

Why Teach This?

- To model how writers get inspiration from mentor texts.
- To demonstrate how mentor texts help us add texture and interest to our own writing.
- To experiment with specific crafting techniques used by writers.

Framing Question

- How can studying our favorite books improve our own writing?

Unit Goals

- Students will choose a mentor text and use it to guide their own writing.
- Students will use writing strategies to add interest to their writing: speech bubbles, detailed illustrations, details about character and setting.

Anchor Texts

- *Knuffle Bunny* by Mo Willems
- *The Napping House* by Audrey Wood
- *Peter's Chair* by Ezra Jack Keats
- *Shortcut* by Donald Crews
- *Where the Wild Things Are* by Maurice Sendak

Resource Sheets

- Speech Bubble Template (Resource 4.2)
- Learning by Imitating Homework Assignment (Resource 4.3)
- Paper Samples (Resources 4.4–4.7)

Unit Assessment Revisiting a Favorite Text to Inspire Writing			STRATEGY
Student name:	EMERGING	DEVELOPING	INDEPENDENT
Adds details about characters and setting in illustrations.			
Varies the location of words on pages in the story.			
Uses speech bubbles in writing.			
Enlarges, darkens, or capitalizes print to convey meaning.			
Titles story thoughtfully.			
Reflects the style of his or her mentor text.			

Stage of the Unit	Focused Instruction You will	Independent Practice Students will
IMMERSION 1 day	• reflect on times when you have learned something by imitating someone.	• draw and write about a time when they learned through imitation of someone else; share with a partner.
IDENTIFICATION 1 day	• articulate what you like about one of your favorite books, *Knuffle Bunny*; reread the book and discuss things you love about it; list things you noticed about the writing and illustrations in the book, creating a class three-column chart.	• write a short story in the style of *Knuffle Bunny*.
GUIDED PRACTICE 12 days	• take a picture walk through *Knuffle Bunny* and study how Mo Willems writes his words on the page; model experimenting with words on the page for your story. • study the way Mo Willems includes clues about setting in his illustrations and photographs; model adding such clues to your story. • study the way Mo Willems tells about his characters in the illustrations; model adding information about your characters by revising your illustrations. • notice the speech bubbles; discuss why the author would use these; model adding speech bubbles in one of your pages to enhance the story.	• experiment with the placement of words on the pages of their story. • add setting clues in their story. • add information about their characters by revising their illustrations. • add speech bubbles to a page or pages in their story.

GUIDED PRACTICE *(continued)*	• study the darkened or enlarged words in *Knuffle Bunny*; discuss why the author would do this and how those words affect the text; model adding darkened or enlarged words to your story.	• add darkened or enlarged words to their story, in the style of *Knuffle Bunny*.
	• study the title *Knuffle Bunny*; ask the students why they think Willems chose that title; study the front cover of *Knuffle Bunny* and discuss what information a reader can learn from it; model revising your title and cover to tell the reader more about your story.	• choose one of their stories and add a thoughtful title and cover illustration.
		• identify their own mentor text that they want to use to guide their writing.
	• model identifying a new mentor text by introducing *Shortcut*, *Where the Wild Things Are*, *Peter's Chair*, *The Napping House*, or some of your favorite texts; think aloud to guide students on what kinds of fiction books make great mentor texts.	• start writing a new story, using their mentor text to guide the placement of the words on the page.
	• read *Shortcut* and model looking at the way the writer puts the words on the page; model writing a new story using your mentor text to guide where you put the words on the page.	• add details about the setting in their story, either through words or through illustrations.
	• examine the setting in *Shortcut*; ask students how the author tells you more about the setting through the words and the illustrations; model adding information about the setting to your story.	• add details about the characters in their book, either through the words or through illustrations.
	• examine the characters in *Shortcut*; ask students how the author tells you about the characters; model adding information about the characters in your story.	• create a captivating title and illustration to catch the reader's attention.
	• model editing your story by focusing on one or two points based on the needs of your class.	
	• study the title and cover of your mentor text, examining why the author chose them to tell readers more about the book; model creating a captivating title and illustration.	

COMMITMENT 1 day	• model meeting with a partner to share your mentor book and your finished story; explain to your partner how the mentor text guided your finished story.	• meet with partners to share their mentor book and their finished stories; explain to each other how the mentor text guided their finished stories.
TOTAL: 15 DAYS		

Structures and Routines

This unit is designed to be taught alongside the reading retelling unit. Stagger the start of the units, beginning with retelling and launching this writing unit approximately a week later. The focus on story elements will naturally support the writing done here.

Partnerships

Immediately after the Focused Instruction, partnerships share their plans for the independent writing time for that day. Writing partnerships will often meet again to read what was written or added to their stories at the conclusion of Independent Practice. When forming partnerships, consider the following areas:

- students' abilities to develop of story structure in writing
- students' abilities to include story details in pictures
- their oral language skills
- their preferred writing topics (actual-event stories or imaginative ones)

Consider the kinds of partnerships you have formed in the past. Throughout a school year we want the students to have a variety of experiences—both heterogeneous and homogeneous working relationships. Both can be successful for this unit.

It is helpful to have partnerships sit next to each other during the Focused Instruction. This allows students to discuss their writing together without having to transition to another location in the room.

Teaching Materials

Knuffle Bunny is the teacher anchor text for the first part of this unit. In the first eight Focused Instruction lessons, we will examine Willems's writing process, study his illustrations, and imitate his writing techniques. For the second half of the unit, another teacher favorite can be used as a mentor text. Choose something that highlights the craft skills taught in the Focused Instruction lessons. Favorite read-aloud books that are perfect for this mentor text unit include *Shortcut* by Donald Crews, *Where the Wild Things Are* by Maurice Sendak, and *Peter's Chair* by Ezra Jack Keats.

Student Materials

Paper

Mo Willems positions the text of *Knuffle Bunny* in playful ways around the page. The paper students use should allow for that same flexibility. There are a few paper choices we give students in this unit:

- blank paper
- picture on the top, lines for text on the bottom
- lines for text on the top, picture on the bottom
- picture in the middle, lines for text on the top and bottom
  (see Resources 4.4–4.7)

Speech Bubble Paper
On Day 6, students imitate Willems's use of speech bubbles in their own stories. Have bubbles of different shapes and sizes available for students to use (see Resource 4.2).

Magazines
Students will go through old magazines in the art center and find photographs that could be the setting for the stories they are writing.

Story Strings
Make Story Strings available for the students while they orally rehearse their stories as well as while they write their stories. These strings provide a visual and tactile representation of story elements. They have proven to be effective and developmentally appropriate for the kindergarten student. Directions for making your own Story Strings are provided in Resource 2.4.

Editing Pencils
Students edit their stories on Day 13 of the unit. It is useful to give young writers colored pencils to make these edits so their work is clearly visible to themselves and you.

Play Center Connections
We launch these play centers after a few days of instruction on *Knuffle Bunny* at writing time.

Art Center
Mo Willems uses photographs as the backdrop for his illustrations in *Knuffle Bunny*. The photos are filled with setting clues and add interest to the book. Gather some old magazines, after Day 4 of the study, use them in the art center. Students find and cut out photographs to use as backgrounds for the stories they are writing in writing time.

Puppet Making
Art materials are available for students to make puppets of the characters in Willems's books. Encourage students to consider characters from any of Willems's books. Students can use these puppets to retell stories in the puppet theater.

Writing Center
Mo Willems frequently uses speech bubbles. His pigeon series and elephant and piggie books are told entirely in this way. Once introduced to them, children are thrilled to use speech bubbles themselves. In the writing center, provide blank speech bubbles of different shapes and sizes. It is the same paper the students use during writing time, beginning on Day 6 of the unit (see Resource 4.2).

Blocks or Legos

Readers must infer the setting of *Knuffle Bunny* by studying details in Willems's photographs. Using blocks, students can build the setting of this book and they can incorporate labels and props as additional setting clues. Students may want to build a different setting for *Knuffle Bunny* and talk about how the story would change if it took place on a farm, for example.

Students build a structure that replicates a scene from their mentor text, *Knuffle Bunny*.

Puppet Theater

Mo Willems has written many books. We make many of them available for students to act out in the puppet theater. The pigeon and elephant and piggie books easily lend themselves to a puppet theater format. Children may want to make character puppets for a book prior to reenacting it in this center.

Stages of the Unit

Immersion

In the beginning of this unit, ask students to reflect on those times when they have learned through imitation. Kindergarteners will talk, draw, and write about those experiences, laying the foundation for studying and imitating the writing of Mo Willems through *Knuffle Bunny*. You are going to demonstrate how you use his text to help you in your own writing.

Identification

Students will notice and name various techniques Willems uses in *Knuffle Bunny*. Create a chart together like this one:

What Mo Willems does in *Knuffle Bunny*:	Why he does this:	Look who tried it!

Guided Practice

Through *Knuffle Bunny*, the class studies the writing techniques Mo Willems uses. Students use *Knuffle Bunny* as their first mentor text with you as their guide. They develop their own stories, guided by the writing and illustrations in *Knuffle Bunny*. For the second half of the unit, students choose their own mentor texts to guide their work on new stories.

Commitment

Kindergarteners examine their writing and their mentor texts carefully, noticing how the mentor texts guided their own stories. Students share these observations with a partner.

Day-by-Day Lessons

DAY 1 Immersion

Focused Instruction

I make fantastic chicken parmesan! I learned how from my dad. I watched him use a mallet to pound the chicken into pieces of equal thickness. I saw how he dipped the chicken from a bowl of egg, to flour, to bread crumbs. I watched carefully and then I did it myself—I imitated what I saw.

How many of you are learning how to tie your shoelaces? Have you been watching a grown-up tie them and then trying it yourself? This is called imitating—doing what you see someone else doing. Imitating is a great way to learn something new.

What else have you learned by imitating? Maybe you learned how to draw a picture by carefully watching someone else do it first. I am going to draw and write about a time when I learned something by imitating someone else.

- Draw a quick picture of watching your dad make chicken parmesan and complete the writing prompt below.

Independent Practice

Today you are going to draw a picture of something you learned by studying and imitating someone else. Fill in the missing words in the sentence below. "I learned how to _____ by studying and imitating _____."

Wrap-Up

Let's go around the room and share what we learned by imitating someone else.

- Students share.

Today for homework you will talk to someone at home about what he or she has learned by imitating. (See Resource 4.3 for a reproducible copy.)

Name _____ Date _____

Learning by Imitating: Homework Assignment

At writing time, we discussed how imitation is a great way to learn something new. We have all learned by imitating others. Today we talked, drew pictures, and wrote about our own experiences of learning through imitating.

Ask a grown-up or sibling at home about what s/he has learned by imitating someone. Talk about what was learned and who he or she learned from.

I talked to _____

She learned how to _____

_____

_____

by imitating _____

_____

RESOURCE 4.3

DAY 2 Identification

Focused Instruction

Yesterday we shared things we learned by imitating someone else. Today we are going to talk about how writers learn by imitating other writers they love. We are going to start with one of my favorite stories: Knuffle Bunny! *We are going to learn how to do things in our own writing by studying and imitating Mo Willems's writing. I am going to reread* Knuffle Bunny *now. You know the story well. Think about what it is that Mo Willems does in his book that you think is really great.*

A teacher uses student photos and copies of their work in the last column of the identification chart.

- Read the book to the class.

What do you like the most about the pictures and words in Knuffle Bunny? *Share one thing you love about the book with the person sitting next to you.*

- Listen in and record students' responses in the first column of the class chart.

What Mo Willems does in Knuffle Bunny:/ *Why he does this:/ Look who tried it!*

Independent Practice

You will write stories in writing time today just like Mo Willems does in this book. Maybe Knuffle Bunny *will give you ideas for the story you want to write today.*

Wrap-Up

I noticed two students whose stories definitely have a little Mo Willems in them.

- Have those two students share their stories.

DAY 3 Guided Practice

Focused Instruction

Today we are going to study the words in Knuffle Bunny. We are going to notice how Mo Willems writes the words on the pages in his book. Today I am going to try moving my words around the page, just like Mo Willems.

- Take a picture walk through *Knuffle Bunny*.
- Model experimenting with the words on the page for your story.

Independent Practice

Let's imitate this writing technique. You can either continue the story you started writing yesterday or begin a new one. As you write, play around with the placement of the words on the page just as Mo Willems does.

- Provide students with paper choices. See Resources 4.4–4.6.

Wrap-Up

Bring one page from your story to the meeting area. It should show how you imitated the way Mo Willems writes his words around the page.

- Students share their writing with a partner.
- Choose a few examples to share with the class.

DAY 4 Guided Practice

Focused Instruction

In reading time we have been learning how to retell the setting of stories—where and when a story takes place.

- Show students the pictures in *Knuffle Bunny*.

What is the setting of Knuffle Bunny*? How do you know? Mo Willems doesn't say it in the words of the story. Willems has put clues in the photographs that tell readers about the setting. What are some of those clues? Why would he do this?*

- Continue to add to the three-column class chart started on Day 2.

Today we are going to imitate this strategy in our own stories.

- Model adding setting clues to the illustrations in your story.

Independent Practice

Today you are going to go back to one of the stories you have written. Add details to your pictures that will tell your reader where the story takes place.

Wrap-Up

Show the person sitting next to you your illustrations and see if he or she can figure out the setting for your story. Remember, your writing partner already knows the setting for your story, so share your work with someone else who is sitting by you.

DAY 5 Guided Practice

Focused Instruction

We know that Mo Willems tells his readers about the setting of Knuffle Bunny *through illustrations and photographs. He is also telling us information about Trixie from his pictures. What can we learn about Trixie from studying the pictures? What do we know about her from the words in the story?*

- Show a few pictures of Trixie to the children. Students should notice Trixie's age and discuss the gender of this character.

Writers use words and illustrations to tell the reader more about their characters. Today we are going to provide some details about our characters by adding to the illustrations.

- Model adding details about the characters in your own story by adding details to your illustrations.

Independent Practice

When you work on your stories today, think about how you can add to the illustrations of your characters to tell more about them—the way Mo Willems does.

Wrap-Up

I want to share the work of two writers in the room who went back to their writing and carefully added details about their characters in their illustrations.

- Share the work of those students with the class. Add students to the three-column chart.

DAY 6 Guided Practice

Focused Instruction

One thing we noticed about Mo Willems's writing is the way he uses speech bubbles. How can speech bubbles help make a story more interesting?

- Study one page in the book and lead children in a discussion about the purpose of using speech bubbles (to let the reader know what a character is saying at a certain point in the story).
- Continue to add to the three-column chart about why Willems uses speech bubbles.

I am going to add some speech bubbles to one of the pages in my story.

- Model adding speech bubbles to one page of your story.

Independent Practice

Now you are going to imitate the way Mo Willems uses speech bubbles in Knuffle Bunny. *Revisit a story you have already written. Reread a page. Think about what the person in your drawing could be saying at that point in the story. Add those words in a speech bubble. I have speech bubble paper for you to use.*

- Students share their speech bubbles with their writing partners during the last five minutes of independent writing time.

Wrap-Up

I noticed two writers who added great speech bubbles to their pages. They were really thinking about the kinds of things their characters might say.

- Share the work of selected students.

DAY 7 Guided Practice

Focused Instruction

You have noticed that Mo Willems plays around with the size and darkness of some of the words in Knuffle Bunny. *Why do you think he does this?*

- Revisit a few pages in the book where print is enlarged or darkened. Examples include where "Trixie realized something" and the speech bubble when "Trixie bawled."

Today I am going to darken a few words in my story or make them bigger the way Mo does.

- Model revising a few words in your story by darkening them or making them bigger.

How does this change my story? What does this tell my reader?

Independent Practice

You may go back to a story you have already written or begin a new one today. Look for the chance to darken a few words or write them bigger the way Mo does and try it.

A student writes in the style of Mo Willems. He writes in different locations on the page, plays with the size and darkness of words and includes a speech bubble: "Then my mommy realized something! The mee mee was gone!"

Wrap-Up

I am going to share with you the writing of a few of your classmates. Let's study the way they used darkened and enlarged words. We will talk about how this improved their stories.

- Add students to the class three-column chart.

DAY 8 Guided Practice

Focused Instruction

Stories have titles and cover illustrations. Let's go back to our anchor text and study its title and cover. Why do you think he chose that title? Today I am going to think of a great title for my story, one that really draws the reader in. And I am going to draw a great cover illustration that makes my reader excited to read my book.

- Model writing a title and drawing a cover illustration to go on the front of the story.

Independent Practice

Today you are going to create a title and draw a cover illustration for one of your stories. Write it on the first page of your story. You can then draw a great cover illustration that makes your reader excited to read your story.

Wrap-Up

- Have a mini-celebration for these pieces. Students can share with one another or invite another class in to hear the stories.

DAY 9 Guided Practice

Focused Instruction

The first mentor text we chose is one of my favorite books. Now you are going to get to choose a favorite book you want to imitate in your writing.

- Model identifying a mentor text by going through some favorite books. Think aloud to guide students on what kind of fiction books make great mentor texts.

I chose a new book to be my mentor text, Shortcut *by Donald Crews (or another book of your choice). I love the way the author writes the words across the pages. This is what I want to do in my writing.*

Independent Practice

Today you are going to go through some of your favorite books and pick one to be your mentor text. Remember it should be a book with writing and pictures that you love. One that you like to read over and over again. One that you want to imitate in your own writing.

- Students go through favorite books and choose one mentor text.

Wrap-Up

I would like us to go around the room and hold up the mentor text we chose. We are not going to explain why we chose it; we are just going to show other writers what we chose.

- Students sit in a circle and take turns holding up the mentor text they chose.

DAY 10 Guided Practice

Focused Instruction

Let's look at the way our new mentor author, Donald Crews, puts the words on the page.

- Examine how *Shortcut* is different than Mo Willems's books and what you notice about the writing.

Donald Crews sometimes writes his words in little groups across the page. But sometimes he writes just one sentence all by itself. Today I am going to try to do that in my writing.

- Model writing one important sentence by itself on the page.

Independent Practice

Look at the way your new mentor author puts the words on the page. You are going to choose something you like about where your author puts the words and try it in your writing.

Wrap-Up

Today I want you to share your new story with your partner. Show your partner the mentor text you chose and take a look at the story you started today. Do they look similar?

DAY 11 Guided Practice

Focused Instruction

Today we are going to look at how your new mentor author writes about or illustrates the setting in the book. In my new mentor text, Shortcut, *Donald Crews uses big, colorful illustrations to show the reader the setting. I am going to try that in my own story today.*

- Model adding color and size to the illustrations in your story.

Independent Practice

Today I want you to look at how your mentor author writes about or illustrates the setting in the book. Find something you like about the way the author shares the setting and imitate it in your own story.

Wrap-Up

I chose a few writers to share their setting illustrations with their model texts today.

- Share a few students' illustrations, also holding up the model text, to show students how the mentor text inspired the student text.

DAY 12 Guided Practice

Focused Instruction

Yesterday we talked about how my mentor author Donald Crews told the reader about the setting by drawing colorful, large illustrations. Today we are going to look at how he tells the reader about the characters in the book. I notice right away that the author draws detailed drawings of the characters on most of the pages.

- Model adding detail to the character illustrations in order to describe the characters more fully.

Independent Practice

Today you are going to look at your mentor text and study how the author tells you about the characters. Try adding details in the illustrations that tell your reader more about the characters in your story.

Wrap-Up

Today I noticed two writers who added great information about their characters in the illustrations.

- Share two students' work that you observed during independent practice.

A teacher uses the SMART board to have students look at ending punctuation on one page of the mentor text.

DAY 13 Guided Practice

Focused Instruction

- Enlarge a page of your story to teach an editing lesson. The content of the lesson should be based on the needs of your class. Possible lessons include spacing between words, ending punctuation, and using a spelling resource. Model reading back through your story and using a red pencil to make changes in the text.

Independent Practice

You are now going to edit your story. I am going to give everyone a red editing pencil. This way the smart editing work you do will stand out.

Wrap-Up

- Write sentences on chart paper or a SMART board, making errors that are similar to what you are noticing in your students' writing. The students help to edit the sentences.

DAY 14 Guided Practice

Focused Instruction

All books have a front cover and title. You added a title and cover illustration for your book inspired by Knuffle Bunny. *Today you are going to look at your new mentor text and figure out how the author wrote a title and created a cover illustration that grab the reader's attention. I notice that Donald Crews wrote a short, one-word title for his book and made a cover illustration that makes me want to know what is going to happen down on the train track.*

- Model writing a title and drawing a cover illustration for your story inspired by *Shortcut*.

Independent Practice

Today I want you to look at the title and cover illustration of your mentor text. You are going to write a title and cover illustration inspired by the text.

Wrap-Up

- Front covers are displayed on table/desktops. Students walk around to admire each other's work.

DAY 15 Commitment

Focused Instruction

Today you are going to meet with a partner to share your mentor book and the story you wrote.

- Model sharing the mentor text and your story with a partner, showing students how you take turns and the kinds of questions you ask each other about your work.

Did you notice how we took turns showing our mentor book and reading our new stories? Today when you meet with your partner, talk about how your mentor book inspired your story. Be sure to tell your partner what you imitated from your mentor book.

Independent Practice

- Students meet in partnerships to share mentor books and their new stories.

Wrap-Up

I am so impressed with the mentor books you chose and the stories you created. Remember that when writers find an author they really love, sometimes they imitate the things they did to help them get better at their own writing. Any time you find a book you really love, you can choose to write your own story that imitates things from that text.

Smooth and Steady

The Reading With Fluency unit and the Blooming Poets writing unit are a nice pairing. There should be a focus on poetry in the reading unit: it's a great way to practice reading fluency and phrasing, but don't read poetry exclusively at this time. That would be very challenging for some of your emergent readers. It's better to read poetry as your read-aloud and also offer it as an option to your readers of all levels during Independent Practice. Then you can do an in-depth study of poetry through the writing unit. Fluency is the goal we are working on in both the reading and writing unit. Mary Lee Prescott-Griffin and Nancy L. Witherell (2008), in their book *Fluency in Focus,* define fluency as not only reading rate and accuracy, but also "phrasing and the use of such elements as pitch, stress, pauses, tone, and expression." Our earlier intensive work on text is now opening up to a broader, more expansive exploration of fluency through the bountiful pleasures of rhythmic language.

Reading With Fluency: Using Chants, Rhymes, and Other Silly Stuff

PROCESS

Why Teach This?

- To teach students specific strategies for reading fluently.
- To model how good readers read aloud fluently.
- To expose students to expressive ways to read and share poetry.

Framing Question

- How do good readers read fluently?

Unit Goals

- Students will read aloud a variety of poems.
- Students will do repeated readings of favorite poems aloud.
- Students will read aloud clearly and expressively.
- Students will attempt phrasing in their favorite poems.

Anchor Texts

- *Arroz Con Leche: Popular Songs and Rhymes from Latin America* by Lulu Delacre
- "Books" by Eloise Greenfield from *In the Land of Words*
- *Little Dog Poems* by Kristine O'Connell George
- "Popsicle" by Joan Bransfield Graham from *Splish Splash*
- "School Bus" and "Sliding Board" by Kay Winters from *Did You See What I Saw?*
- "Things" and "Rope Rhyme" by Eloise Greenfield from *Honey I Love and Other Poems*

Unit Assessment Reading With Fluency: Using Chants, Rhymes, and Other Silly Stuff

PROCESS

Student name:	EMERGING	DEVELOPING	INDEPENDENT
Reads poems (at level) fluently.			
Does repeated readings of poems to increase fluency.			
Reads aloud clearly and expressively.			
Attempts phrasing in favorite poems.			

Stage of the Unit	Focused Instruction You will	Independent Practice Students will
IMMERSION 2 days	• read anchor poems aloud (e.g., "Things" by Eloise Greenfield), reading with fluency, expression, and distinct phrasing; ask students what they noticed and what they liked about the way you read.	• choose from a variety of familiar poems (of different levels) with a partner; read poems to each other aloud.
IDENTIFICATION 1 day	• read a poem from *Little Dog Poems* and ask students what they have noticed about the way you have been reading the poems; make a chart of the things you have done while reading that make the poem sound great (e.g., reading slowly to savor the words, changing your voice for different parts of the poem, reading the poems in sections or phrases).	• choose one of the things on the chart to practice with their partners when reading familiar poems aloud.
GUIDED PRACTICE 6 days	• choose a poem that you love as a "favorite"; explain how you chose it and that you want to work on this one before sharing it with a partner; model reading the poem aloud repeatedly to practice the words and the way you will read it; emphasize that good readers practice what they're going to share so their reading sounds great (two days of instruction).	• choose a poem they love as a favorite; practice rereading it by themselves; read their favorite poems aloud to a partner at the end of Independent Practice. • practice reading their favorite poem aloud, thinking about using clear, expressive, loud speaking voices; read their favorite poem aloud to a partner at the end of Independent Practice (repeat this process for three days).

GUIDED PRACTICE (continued)	• read a song/poem from *Arroz Con Leche: Popular Songs and Rhymes from Latin America* and model what appropriate read aloud voices sound like as opposed to voices that do not help listeners enjoy the poem; model reading your favorite poem clearly and expressively, thinking aloud about how you will read it first.	• practice reading their favorite poem (or a new poem) and thinking about the phrases, or parts, of the poem by examining punctuation; read their favorite poem aloud to a partner at the end of Independent Practice.
	• model reading another poem aloud from *Little Dog Poems* in one long phrase; explain that good readers break a poem up into phrases, or parts, to help the listener understand (two days of instruction).	
	• using a large text, show students that many phrases are indicated by line breaks; model reading the same poem in phrases, following the line breaks.	
COMMITMENT 1 day	• choose one favorite poem that you love to read aloud; emphasize that it is one you have practiced and you feel really comfortable reading aloud; model reading it for the class in a clear, expressive, audible voice.	• choose one favorite poem that they love to read aloud; practice reading their poem aloud, thinking about keeping their voices clear, expressive, and audible; read their favorite, practiced poems for the class at the end of Independent Practice.
TOTAL: 10 DAYS		

The Lilt of Language

One of the best ways to foster fluency in our youngest writers is through the art and music of poetry. The rhythms, the silences, the lilt of the language carry us along like a tide. This companion unit is playful and at the same time, serious. Poetry is joyous and bouncy, but also holds big ideas and emotions, even for our youngest writers. Add pep to your work in fluency with this next unit in poetry writing.

Blooming Poets: A Writing Unit   GENRE

Why Teach This?

- To expose students to the look and sound of poetry.
- To instill in students a love and appreciation of poetry.
- To teach students techniques poets use when writing poems.

Framing Question

- What is poetry?
- How can we write our poetry?

Unit Goals

- Students will develop an appreciation for poetry—recognizing its sounds, rhythms, imagery, and playful language.
- Students will use a variety of techniques when writing poetry.

Anchor Texts

- *Arroz Con Leche: Popular Songs and Rhymes from Latin America* by Lulu Delacre
- "Behold the Bold Umbrellaphant" by Jack Prelutsky from *Behold the Bold Umbrellaphant*
- "Books," "Nathaniel's Rap," and "New Baby Poem" by Eloise Greenfield from *In the Land of Words*
- *Little Dog Poems* by Kristine O'Connell George
- "Popsicle" by Joan Bransfield Graham from *Splish Splash*
- "School Bus" and "Sliding Board" by Kay Winters from *Did You See What I Saw?*
- "Things" and "Rope Rhyme" by Eloise Greenfield from *Honey I Love and Other Love Poems*

Unit Assessment Blooming Poets: A Writing Unit			GENRE
Student name:	EMERGING	DEVELOPING	INDEPENDENT
Uses observations, memories, feelings, imagination, and wonderings as a source of ideas for poems (the Four Prompts).			
Creates poems with a rhythm and beat.			
Uses descriptive language to paint a picture in the reader's mind.			
Writes meaningful poems using simple language.			
Uses space and structure to convey the meaning of a poem.			

Stage of the Unit	Focused Instruction You will	Independent Practice Students will
IMMERSION 2 days	• read various anchor poems aloud (e.g., "Things" by Eloise Greenfield and "Behold the Bold Umbrellaphant" by Jack Prelutsky); ask students what they notice; reflect on how poems are different from other types of writing; model writing poems inspired by the anchor poems.	• write a variety of poems from their imagination or inspired by anchor poems.
IDENTIFICATION 1 day	• read a poem from *Little Dog Poems* and ask students what they have noticed about the poems they have heard; emphasize that poets use words differently to express their ideas and feelings: • poetry sounds different (has rhythm and a beat, poets say a lot with a little); • poetry looks different (white space, shape poems); • poets use descriptive words to paint a picture in the reader's mind.	• write a poem using one or more of the features mentioned at left (this first attempt will be kept for assessment of growth and understanding).

GUIDED PRACTICE 6 days	• read "Nathaniel's Rap" and "New Baby Poem" by Eloise Greenfield; read the poet's notes on where she found inspiration for each of her poems (imagination and wonderings); explain and model how writers get their ideas from their imagination and things they wonder about. • model how poets choose different kinds of paper to fit the poem they want to write; introduce the various kinds of paper and explain how they might fit different kinds of poems. • read "Popsicle" by Joan Bransfield Graham and "Rope Rhyme" by Eloise Greenfield, noticing the rhythm of each poem; model writing a poem that uses rhythm or has a beat. • read "School Bus" by Kay Winters and reflect on where the poet might have gotten the idea for this poem; emphasize how poets get their ideas from their memories and things they notice; model writing a poem inspired by a special memory or something you notice. • reread "School Bus" by Kay Winters; notice how poets use descriptive words; model writing a poem that uses descriptive words to paint a picture in the reader's head. • read "Morning Nap" by Kristine O'Connell George and "Sliding Board" by Kay Winters and notice how the poets write the words on the page in a specific shape that supports the meaning of the poem; model writing a shape poem that uses words on the page to support the meaning.	• write poems inspired by their imagination or something they wonder about. • choose different kinds of paper to fit the poems they want to write. • write poems that use rhythm or a beat. • write poems inspired by special memories or things they notice. • write poems that use descriptive words to paint pictures in a reader's head. • experiment with the use of white space and shape in their poems.

COMMITMENT 2 days	• go through the folder of poems you have written in this unit; think aloud while rereading your poems to choose one that is special to you; model reading your poem to a partner and explaining to her why this poem is so special. • model how poets present their poetry to a group, reading aloud in a clear, loud voice with expression.	• go through their writing folders to select one poem that is special to them; meet with a partner to read their poems and explain why they are so special. • share their special poem in a class celebration ("poetry slam"); read in a clear, loud voice with expression.
TOTAL: 11 DAYS		

Solve Those Word Puzzles

At this time of year, you may have readers at all points along the spectrum: some who are reading fluently, others who are just beginning to recognize sounds in letter clusters. It is a delightful yet puzzling time for many teachers. Taking time to do the strategic work of becoming a reader and writer is a way to address some of these issues head-on: helping children find strategies for getting unstuck, both with spelling and idea generation and revision. These all involve using materials wisely and well. This is your kindergarteners' chance to carry a grown-up toolbox for strategies, too.

Deepening Understanding: Essential Reading Strategies

STRATEGY

Why Teach This?

- To teach students a variety of word-solving strategies to use when reading.
- To teach students how to improve their reading comprehension.

Framing Questions

- What do good readers do when they read?
- How do they figure out words they do not know?

Unit Goals

- Students will use prior knowledge to get their minds ready to read.
- Students will use a variety of print strategies.
- Students will check to make sure they understand what they've read.
- Students will begin to self-correct during reading.

Anchor Texts

- *My Kindergarten* by Rosemary Wells
- *Olivia Saves the Circus* by Ian Falconer
- *Señor Cat's Romance and Other Favorite Stories from Latin America* by Lucia M. Gonzalez
- *Stellaluna* by Janell Cannon

Unit Assessment Deepening Understanding: Essential Reading Strategies			STRATEGY
Student name:	EMERGING	DEVELOPING	INDEPENDENT
Uses prior knowledge to get ready to read.			
Uses picture clues to figure out unknown words.			
Uses beginning sounds to figure out unknown words.			
Uses ending sounds to figure out unknown words.			
Checks for meaning while reading: "Does this make sense?"			
Begins to cross-check while reading, using a variety of strategies.			
Begins to self-correct while reading.			

Stage of the Unit	Focused Instruction You will	Independent Practice Students will
IMMERSION 1 day	• read *Olivia Saves the Circus* and discuss how readers build a story in their mind as they read; explain that just as builders have a toolbox for their tools, readers also have a special reader's toolbox; explain that these tools are the strategies or things they do to help them figure out tough words and to understand the story; think aloud while reading a familiar text and demonstrate what you do if you do not know a word and how you check if you understand what you are reading.	• read independently and notice what strategies they use when they get stuck on a word they do not know. (Students may begin to imitate the strategies modeled in the Focused Instruction.)
IDENTIFICATION 1 day	• read a story from *Señor Cat's Romance* and identify and chart the strategies readers use when they do not know a word (prior knowledge, picture clues, sounds they know); model using the various strategies.	• read independently and notice what strategies they use when they get stuck on a word they do not know. (Students may choose to use one of the modeled strategies to help them.)

GUIDED PRACTICE 4 days	• model getting your mind ready to read by thinking about what you already know about the topic. • use *Stellaluna* to model how readers use picture clues to figure out unfamiliar words in a familiar anchor text. • reread *Stellaluna* and demonstrate how readers figure out words by making the sound of the first letter in a familiar anchor text. • read a second story from *Señor Cat's Romance* and demonstrate how readers use the last letter of the word to help figure out a word (teach only when students are using beginning letter sounds consistently). • demonstrate how readers cross-check during reading (verify that they are reading a word correctly) by using a variety of word strategies. • use *My Kindergarten* to model how readers ask, "Does this make sense?" during reading to check their comprehension and understanding.	• read independently, practicing getting their minds ready to read by thinking about what they already know. • read independently, using picture clues to figure out unfamiliar words. • read independently, using beginning letter sounds to figure out unknown words. • read independently, using ending letter sounds to figure out unfamiliar words. • read independently, practicing cross-checking during reading using a variety of word strategies. • read independently, asking themselves, "Does this make sense?" while they are reading to check their understanding of the story.
COMMITMENT 1 day	• identify a method good readers use to figure out the meaning of what they're reading and how they figure out words they don't know; draw a picture of yourself using that strategy (you may include thinking bubbles to explain your thinking).	• draw a picture of themselves using a word-attack or comprehension strategy (students can hang these pictures around the room to remind themselves how to understand what they read).
TOTAL: 7 DAYS		

Deepening Meaning: Essential Writing Strategies

STRATEGY

Why Teach This?

- To teach students specific strategies to keep them writing after they are "finished."
- To emphasize the importance of rereading your writing and adding on to a story with details.
- To encourage students to be self-sufficient during independent writing time.

Framing Question

- How do writers add on to stories that are finished?

Unit Goals

- Students will visualize the story they wrote.
- Students will reread their writing and add more details to an illustration.
- Students will reread their writing and add more details to the writing.
- Students will reread their writing and add on to a writing piece by adding more pages and text.

Anchor Texts

- *Black Cat* by Christopher Myers
- *Señor Cat's Romance and Other Favorite Stories from Latin America* by Lucia M. Gonzalez
- *Snowy Surprise* by Amy Hest

Unit Assessment Deepening Meaning: Essential Writing Strategies			STRATEGY
Student name:	EMERGING	DEVELOPING	INDEPENDENT
Visualizes a story.			
Rereads writing when he or she is "finished."			
Adds details to an illustration after he or she is "finished."			
Adds details to writing after he or she is "finished."			
Adds pages and text to their writing.			

Stage of the Unit	Focused Instruction You will	Independent Practice Students will
IMMERSION 1 day	• write a story and announce that you are finished; think aloud and model rereading your writing and add to both the drawing and writing.	• write independently and reflect on strategies they can use when they feel done with a piece of writing to add to it.
IDENTIFICATION 1 day	• model revisiting writing from the previous day and add another page to the story; ask students to name the strategies a writer can use to add to his or her work.	• use the strategies listed to make a piece of writing complete.
GUIDED PRACTICE 2 days	• revisit a previous piece of writing; reread it and decide that you will visualize the story to make sure you included all the important details; after modeling visualization, decide to add more details based on what you visualized; emphasize that students can add on to illustrations with more details when they are "done." (*Black Cat* or *Snowy Surprise* can be used as example texts.) • read *Señor Cat's Romance* and imagine how the story could be extended; visualize a "completed" story and model deciding that it can be extended; model choosing a type of writing paper to use for the addition of your story.	• write independently; reread their writing and visualize to add details to their illustrations. • write independently; reread and visualize their story if they finish it; choose additional kinds of writing paper if they want to extend their story.
COMMITMENT 1 day	• share with students the three ways you added on to work that was "finished" this week. Show the add-on that you are most proud of and describe how it helps tell your story.	• choose which add-on they are most proud of and which helped them tell their story; share this story with a partner.
TOTAL: 5 DAYS		

From Winter to Spring

The kindergartener is entering the joyous season of spring. She is truly a part of the school community now. She has deepened her reading and writing strategies. Now she is ready for the world of nonfiction reading and writing. She will make books and share her knowledge with friends. As the year draws to a close, she will take flight in her imagination. She dreams of fictional stories which will propel her down the pages, and she will end the year with collections of her writing and evidence of her reading that will make her proud.

Chapter 5

SPRING

The Kindergartener as Bold Explorer

"A loudspeaker blares out the address of the fire, and the firefighters go into action. They slide down brass poles to the ground floor, where the fire engines are, and hurry into their fire-fighting gear. They take their positions on the engines. The big trucks roar out of the firehouse."
—from *Fire! Fire!* by Gail Gibbons

The kindergartener is indeed a bold explorer. In this season we celebrate this with units of study that engage our students on many levels. We study nonfiction together as readers and writers, and build fluency through exposure to new texts and with an introduction to new conventions of print. Everything is new, and everything is fresh. There is no end to the delights of exploration. Join us as we share with you these units in the last season of the year, sending your students off to first grade fortified, bold, and brave.

SPRING UNITS

SPOTLIGHT on Genre

- Exploring Many Worlds: Nonfiction Reading
- Knowing and Sharing: Nonfiction Writing

There are a few great writers who have been able to write across several genres. E. B. White comes to mind. He wrote the classic children's books *Charlotte's Web*, *Trumpet of the Swan*, and *Stuart Little*. He wrote small humorous snippets for *The New Yorker* in the Talk of the Town column. And, he cowrote the seminal how-to guide to grammar, *The Elements of Style*. White was the rare genius who could accommodate all genres, fitting his observations, his wonderings, his memory, and his imagination into a wide variety of "containers." Great ideas are like water, flowing clear—a stream. Genre is a container we use to hold those ideas. The ideas are the same, but they look different depending on the container that holds them. Loneliness inside a poem, for example, looks different from loneliness inside a science fiction novel. Courage inside a biography looks different from courage inside a letter. A clear idea, held inside the right container can change someone's mind, even someone's life. See pages 47–61 in my book *The Complete 4 for Literacy* for a more detailed description of the elements and categories of genre and the importance of these units to the lives of our students. They are seeking to clarify, extend and share from their own stream of ideas.

Pam Allyn

EARLY FALL · LATE FALL · WINTER · SPRING

Inquire, Explore, Learn!

Kindergarteners are inquiring, vividly curious, deeply passionate learners. They can study a pebble or a beetle with the kind of fascination older children would reserve for a glacier or an elephant. At this time of year, your students are ready for a more lengthy unit in nonfiction reading, with a companion unit in writing. They love to explore, and this unit provides them the opportunity to explore interests through the pages of books and in developing their own ideas. Nonfiction books in the primary classroom provide critical exposure to the genre (Palmer & Stewart, 2003). For the rest of their lives, our students will be reading and writing and expected to feel a sense of mastery in this genre. Now is the time to expose them to it in ways that will help them understand that the nonfiction reader and writer in the world is curious and passionate, just like them.

Exploring Many Worlds: Nonfiction Reading

GENRE

Why Teach This?

- To expose students to the genre of nonfiction.
- To teach students genre characteristics of nonfiction.
- To give students the opportunity to explore their interests through books.

Framing Questions

- What is nonfiction?
- How is nonfiction different from stories and poems?

Unit Goals

- Students will distinguish between fiction and nonfiction.
- Students will read and gain information from nonfiction text features.
- Students will understand that nonfiction books are a way to explore interests, passions, and questions.

Anchor Texts

- *Actual Size* by Steve Jenkins
- *Bats* by Gail Gibbons
- *Bears* by Daniel Wood
- *Busy as a Bee* by Melvin Berger (big book)
- *Chameleons Are Cool* by Martin Jenkins
- *Dinosaur ABC* by Roger Priddy
- *Farm Animals* by DK Readers
- *Fire! Fire!* by Gail Gibbons
- *Garden Friends* by DK Readers
- *Growing Vegetable Soup* by Lois Ehlert
- *Jazz on a Saturday Night* by Leo Dillon
- *Little Bear* by Else Homelund Minarik
- *Red Leaf, Yellow Leaf* by Lois Ehlert

- *Spiders* by Gail Gibbons
- *Stellaluna* by Janell Cannon
- *Stone Soup* by Jon Murth
- *The Story of Ruby Bridges* by Robert Coles
- *The Very Busy Spider* by Eric Carle
- *Who Lives in the Sea?* by Sylvia M. James (big book)
- *Why Do Leaves Change Color?* by Betsy Maestro

Resource Sheet

- Parent Letter (Resource 5.1)

Unit Assessment Exploring Many Worlds: Nonfiction Reading			GENRE
Student name:	EMERGING	DEVELOPING	INDEPENDENT
Distinguishes between fiction and nonfiction.			
Engages in prereading strategies appropriate to nonfiction texts.			
Identifies nonfiction text features.			
Understands the purpose of various text features.			
Accesses information from text features.			
Prepares for book-partner conversation.			
Expresses thoughts and ideas about a book clearly.			

Stage of the Unit	Focused Instruction You will	Independent Practice Students will
IMMERSION 5 days	• discuss the varied purposes for reading nonfiction. • use *The Story of Ruby Bridges* and *Fire! Fire!* to show how there are many kinds of nonfiction to be read for many purposes. • discuss the idea that nonfiction readers explore their interests and answer questions in nonfiction books; create a chart of some of the class's interests. • explore the differences between fiction and nonfiction texts.	• sketch and write about something they learned from reading nonfiction. • sketch someone from their life who reads nonfiction—write who and what they read. • browse through nonfiction books. • sort books into two piles: fiction and nonfiction.

IDENTIFICATION 1 day	• read *Who Lives in the Sea?* and chart the differences between fiction and nonfiction texts; discuss how fiction and nonfiction books look and sound different.	• explore the nonfiction books in tabletop baskets.
GUIDED PRACTICE 12 days	• compare *Vegetable Soup* and *Stone Soup* and discuss how the fiction and nonfiction texts are similar and different. • use *Little Bear* and *Bears* to discuss the similarities and differences between using reading strategies with nonfiction and using them with fiction. • use *Garden Friends* to model how to preread nonfiction by looking at the cover of a book. • read *Fire! Fire!* and model how to take a picture walk through a nonfiction text. • read *Farm Animals* and model how to find clues to tricky words. • read *Garden Friend* and model studying and reading nonfiction text features: photographs, illustrations, and diagrams. • model using print strategies for reading captions. • think aloud while reading; record the ways nonfiction readers respond to their books. • read *Busy as a Bee* and demonstrate making a sketch on sticky notes to remind yourself of your thinking. • model using the word "because" to extend the way we talk about our thinking. • choose one or two of the nonfiction titles and demonstrate retelling a nonfiction book: title, topic, and opinion of the book.	• compare a fiction and nonfiction book with a partner. • study the front cover of books as a prereading strategy. • take a picture walk in their nonfiction books. • study the text features in their nonfiction books. • mark places where they responded to their nonfiction books and share their thinking with partners. • use the word "because" when they are talking about nonfiction books. • make a sketch on sticky notes and talk about their thinking with partners. • retell a book to a partner: title, topic, opinion of the book, two places where they used sticky notes to respond to the book.

COMMITMENT 2 days	• guide students through a reflection and listing of topics and interests they want to read more about. • guide students through a reflection of how they have grown as readers and what they know about nonfiction books.	• choose a nonfiction book of interest from the school library to bring back to the classroom. • orally reflect on their new learning and growth as readers as a result of this unit; share a favorite nonfiction book with a friend.
TOTAL: 20 DAYS		

Getting Started

These reading and writing units are designed to allow students to pursue their own interests while learning about the genre of nonfiction. The reading unit begins approximately five days before the writing unit. This immersion period gives our students a general understanding of the genre before we ask them to write nonfiction.

Structures and Routines

During the first half of the unit, rotate tabletop baskets from table to table every two days. For the last two weeks, reorganize the books by topic and have students read from a topic of their choice. During play-center time, put index cards in the art center for students to use to make illustrations that correspond to the topic of the books. These will serve as labels for the book baskets.

Partnerships

More than with any other genre, when our students read nonfiction they come across information they want to share immediately. Seeing the photograph of an octopus wrapped around a rock or a goliath spider in actual size is exciting for our youngest readers.

This unit is a wonderful opportunity to form interest-based partnerships.

Setting Up Tabletop Baskets

As you are gathering books to put in your tabletop baskets, make sure to include a variety of topics, levels of text difficulty, and text features.

Possible topic baskets:

- Animals: sea creatures, reptiles, birds, mammals (if you have enough books, each of these animal categories could be its own basket)
- Weather
- Insects
- Vehicles
- Places
- Sports

Differentiation

You now have a number of students who are beginning to read. Ideally, you will have a collection of leveled nonfiction books for these students to read during independent reading time.

Publishers of leveled nonfiction books:

• National Geographic School Publishing—Windows on Literacy series

• Mondo Publishing

• Sundance Publishing—Wonder Books series

• Teacherwide.com—Nonfiction Leveled Readers

• Newbridge Publishing—this publisher offers versions of each book at three different levels

• Scholastic Readers—Time to Discover series

Play Center Connections

While students are engaged in nonfiction reading and writing, it is the perfect time to launch a nonfiction focus to your play centers, perhaps incorporating the science or social studies curriculum. One kindergarten teacher we know, attentive to the New York State social-studies curriculum, which requires that kindergarteners learn about their community, created a unit on trains and Grand Central Station (many of her students have parents who commute into the city to work). The students are familiar with the commuter train: the station is in the center of their town and they watch the trains go by on an elevated track many times a day. This teacher plans the unit to coincide with her nonfiction reading and writing unit.

Students' work in play centers each day focuses on some aspect of the train theme. In the art center, students make a large train out of a refrigerator box using photographs and books about trains as resources. In the block area, students build a train station and label it with important words. In the writing center, students write nonfiction books about trains and Grand Central Station. In dramatic play, students set up a ticket booth and write and sell tickets to customers.

Science Center

If you do not have a science center in your classroom at other times of the year, now is a good time to open one. This center typically focuses on one topic. Students learn about the topic from observations and hands-on exploration. You may want to gather objects from outside that represent the season of the year (different branches with buds on them, spring flowers, etc.) or use a class pet as possible science center topics. We make magnifying glasses available (which the kids love!) as well as two or three books on the topic we're studying. We also put paper out on clipboards so students can draw and write about what they are observing and learning. As students are drawing their observations in this center, we encourage them to use the nonfiction text features they are learning about in reading and writing, such as diagrams and zoom-in boxes.

Stages of the Unit

Immersion

Engage students in a discussion about the varied purposes for this genre and have them identify people in their lives who read nonfiction. Students read nonfiction books that are organized in tabletop baskets. These books do not have to be on the students' independent reading levels: they are reading above and below their levels in this unit as they explore their passions and make connections to the books. On the last Immersion day, students sort a mixed collection of books into piles of fiction and nonfiction. A parent letter can be sent home at this time (see Resource 5.1).

Identification

Identify how nonfiction books are different from fiction. Characteristics used to identify genre include facts versus story and the special text features of nonfiction.

Guided Practice

Model prereading strategies. Students learn how to use various text features, and discuss nonfiction topics with partners, using the text as a support.

Commitment

Students reflect on what they have learned in this unit. They recall what they now know about nonfiction books and what they can do as readers.

Day-by-Day Lessons

DAY 1 Immersion

Focused Instruction

When I want to learn more about something, I read nonfiction. What kinds of things do you want to learn more about?

- Students share what they like to learn about.

Reading nonfiction helps us to learn about things we love. Can you recall a time you read a book because you wanted to learn more about something you loved?

Independent Practice

Draw a picture of something you learned about from reading a nonfiction book. Add words related to the topic.

Wrap-Up

- Students share their drawings and anecdotes.

DAY 2 Immersion

Focused Instruction

There are many kinds of nonfiction. Today, we are going to look at Fire! Fire! *and* The Story of Ruby Bridges *to learn about different types of nonfiction texts.*

- Show students different forms of nonfiction, such as newspapers, magazines, and instructional texts.

Independent Practice

Draw a picture of someone in your life who reads nonfiction. Include the form of nonfiction that he or she reads. Write the name of the person in your drawing and the nonfiction he or she is reading—a newspaper or a magazine or a book.

Wrap-Up

- Invite a guest from your school community to discuss his or her nonfiction reading life. Ask the guest to bring examples of what he or she is reading.

DAY 3 Immersion

Focused Instruction

Readers read nonfiction books to explore their interests and to answer questions about them. Let's chart what we are most interested in.

Independent Practice

See if you can find a book that matches an interest you have. Maybe you will come across a book that gets you interested in something new.

- Students browse nonfiction book baskets to find books that match their interests.

Wrap-Up

Let's return to our chart and add more interests based on some of the books you were browsing.

DAY 4 Immersion

Focused Instruction

I have with me a few nonfiction books I am reading at home. I am reading about dogs because I am going to get one and I need to know what to do to take care of it. Readers of nonfiction read to answer questions and learn new ideas. What questions do you have about something?

- Read aloud from *Jazz on a Saturday Night* and discuss what you can learn from the text.

Independent Practice

As you look through the books in the tabletop basket today, think about what leads you to a particular book. Do you have a question you want to answer? Is there a book on a topic you do not know anything about but would like to learn about it?

Wrap-Up

- Choose one or two students to bring a book to the meeting area and talk about why they choose that particular book.

DAY 5 Immersion

Focused Instruction

We know that nonfiction books teach real information. We also know that storybooks, or fiction books, tell a story. Today we are going to look through piles of books and sort them into two groups: fiction (storybooks) and nonfiction (books that teach). I look through this book and think about whether it is fiction or nonfiction. Let's notice all the ways we can tell the difference.

Independent Practice

In your tabletop baskets, you will find both fiction and nonfiction books. Work with your partner to look through a book and decide whether it is fiction or nonfiction. Make two piles, one with fiction books and the other with nonfiction. I will give each partnership two sticky notes—one says "fiction" and the other "nonfiction." You will use these notes to label your piles.

Wrap-Up

Each partnership should come to our meeting area with two books: one fiction and one nonfiction. You will get a chance to share how you knew which pile to put each book in when you were sorting.

DAY 6 Identification

Focused Instruction

How does a reader recognize a nonfiction book? What makes it different from a storybook? Let's continue to chart our ideas.

- Read from *Who Lives in the Sea?* and chart some characteristics of a nonfiction book.

Independent Practice

As you read from tabletop baskets, see if our descriptions of fiction and nonfiction match your books. When we come back together at the Wrap-Up, you will have an opportunity to add to our description.

Wrap-Up

Let's continue to add to our description of what nonfiction is.

DAY 7 Guided Practice

Focused Instruction

Today we are going to continue adding to our chart by listing how nonfiction looks different from fiction. Here is a nonfiction big book that we read together earlier in the year, Growing Vegetable Soup *by Lois Ehlert. As I read it again, think about how it looks different from our book* Stone Soup.

What looks different about it? Let's list some text features together.

Independent Practice

- Students read and explore texts.

Wrap-Up

- Two students share the text features they discovered in their reading.

DAY 8 Guided Practice

Focused Instruction

Let's look at two books about the same topic. One is a book we love called Little Bear *by Else Minarik. The other is a book called* Bears *by Daniel Wood. I am going to browse through these books. Let us think about how they are the same and how they are different. Let's chart our observations.*

- Other pairs of fiction and nonfiction titles include:

Fiction titles		Nonfiction titles
Red Leaf, Yellow Leaf by Lois Ehlert	with	*Why Do Leaves Change Color?* by Betsy Maestro
Stellaluna by Janell Cannon	with	*Bats* by Gail Gibbons
The Very Busy Spider by Eric Carle	with	*Spiders* by Gail Gibbons

Independent Practice

Today in Independent Practice, I have given each partnership a set of fiction and nonfiction books on the same subject. Take some time to browse through them and see what you notice. How are they the same and how are they different?

Wrap-Up

- One or two partners share about their text sets and what they noticed.

DAY 9 Guided Practice

Focused Instruction

When a reader studies the cover of a nonfiction book, he gets clues as to what the book is about. He is reminded of things he already knows about the particular topic, and it usually makes him think of a few questions about the topic. Let's look at one of our nonfiction books, *Garden Friends. What do you think this book may be about? What questions do you immediately have as a reader?*

- Students brainstorm questions.

Independent Practice

Today when you look at books in your basket, start by studying the front cover. Discuss with your partner: What might this book be about? What do I already know about this topic? What questions do I have?

- Students ask questions with their partners before they start browsing the books.

Wrap-Up

Today you learned about the thinking nonfiction readers do—thinking about what the book may be about and thinking about what you may already know about the topic.

- Two partnerships share.

DAY 10 Guided Practice

Focused Instruction

Nonfiction readers often turn pages slowly, looking at the pictures or photographs. Readers of nonfiction books think to themselves, "What am I learning on this page?" rather than thinking about a story from page to page. Watch me as I take a picture walk through this nonfiction book, Fire! Fire! *by Gail Gibbons. Let's practice how we ask questions as we read.*

- Chart students' questions as you read.

Independent Practice

- Students read, noting questions on sticky notes as they go.

Wrap-Up

- Students share questions.

DAY 11 Guided Practice

Focused Instruction

Today we are going to learn how to gain information from studying photographs and illustrations. The words in your books are telling information about a topic, and the photograph and illustrations are telling information as well.

- Read *Busy as a Bee.*

Independent Practice

- Students read and note photographs and illustrations that teach them something.

Wrap-Up

- Students share what they've learned from their reading.

DAY 12 Guided Practice

Focused Instruction

You noticed that some nonfiction books have labels in them. You know all about labels from our study earlier in the year. We are going to look at this book, Farm Animals, *which has many labels. We will practice finding clues that enable us to read the words.*

- Use an enlarged text with captions to practice using the three cueing systems for reading unknown words.

Independent Practice

When you read your books, remember to hunt for and find the clues that will help you to read tricky words.

Wrap-Up

Give me a thumbs-up if you found a label in your book today. Who would like to share what their label said?

DAY 13 Guided Practice

Focused Instruction

Our book Garden Friends *has many diagrams. A diagram is a labeled drawing that teaches us about the parts of something.*

Independent Practice

If you find a diagram in your book today, try to read the labels. Remember to find the clues in the picture and words that will enable you to read the word.

- Differentiating Instruction
  - Strong readers can be given *Dinosaur ABC* by Rodger Priddy, which contains diagrams with more descriptive labels. "Small head" and "sharp claws" are two examples of the kinds of labels found in this book.

Wrap-Up

We studied labels in books earlier in the year. How are labels different from diagrams? How are they the same?

- Find a partnership to share the work they did reading a diagram or label.

DAY 14 Guided Practice

Focused Instruction

- Take this day to teach a lesson based on the particular needs of your students. Perhaps you have noticed that your kindergarteners are not using their pre-reading strategies and you would like to review those again. Maybe you want to teach another print-based lesson, using a more sophisticated diagram. You may also want to use this day to switch to topic-specific book baskets and have students choose which topic they would like to read about for the next few days.

DAY 15 Guided Practice

Focused Instruction

Now that you are reading your nonfiction books, the energy level in our room has been great! I love that you have been so excited about what you are reading. I hear you sharing with your partners: "That is so cool!" "That is just like..." "I wonder..." When you react that way to your books it means you are really thinking about the information on the page, and that is strong reading! I am going to show you how you can use a sticky note to mark a place you want to share with your reading partner. We are going to call these sticky notes "thinking squares" because they mark the smart thinking you are doing in your books. Watch me as I read this page in our big book Who Lives in the Sea?

- Think aloud as you read a page in a big book and react to it in some way—surprise, excitement, disbelief, being reminded of something else, and so on.

I am going to take this thinking square and put it on this page because I definitely want to talk to my partner about the thinking I am doing here!

Independent Practice

Everyone is going to get one thinking square to use in their books today. You will have 10 minutes to read independently and then you will meet with your partner. When you find a part that you really want to share with your partner, put your thinking square there. Before meeting with your partner, think about what you will say about that part in your book.

Wrap-Up

- Share an anecdote of a partnership sharing parts in their books with each other.

DAY 16 Guided Practice

Focused Instruction

Yesterday you used a thinking square to mark a place in your book you wanted to share with your partner. Today I am going to continue reading Who Lives in the Sea? *the big book I started yesterday. Listen to the ways I think about the information on the pages. Listen to how I use the word "because" to talk about my thinking: "Wow. Look at this orange starfish. This surprises me because I did not know starfish could be this color."*

- Model thinking aloud for the students. It is preferable to read from an enlarged text and one that is new to the students. You may model being surprised by information in a book or perhaps it reminds you of prior knowledge. Use the word "because" when explaining your thinking.

Independent Practice

Everyone will get two thinking squares today. Read independently for 10 minutes and mark two places where you want to share your thinking in your book with your partner. Then you will meet with your partner and take turns sharing and talking about your books. Try to use the word "because" to explain your thinking.

- While conferring with students and partnerships, record the things they are saying about their books. Prompt children to use the word "because" to stretch their thinking.

Wrap-Up

You are talking about your books in smart ways. These are some of the things I heard you say about your books.

- Share orally or on a chart the comments students made about their books.

DAY 17 Guided Practice

Focused Instruction

You have been using thinking squares to mark the places in your books where you have done some thinking that you want to share with your partner. I have noticed that sometimes you forget what you want to say when you are sharing with your partners. Today we are going to decide on sketches that you can make on your thinking squares to remind yourself of what you wanted to say about a particular page. Let's read Busy as a Bee *and practice!*

This chart shows some of the ways you are reacting to the information in your books:

| This is interesting. |
| I am wondering about something. |
| This reminds me of something. |

Are there other ways you are thinking about your books that are not shown on our chart?

We are going to decide together what sketches we can make that would remind us of the particular thinking we are doing in our books.

Independent Practice

Everyone will get two thinking squares to use in their books today. Draw a sketch to remind yourself of what you want to say on that page. When you meet with your partner, remember to use the word "because" to explain your thinking.

Wrap-Up

- Choose students to share their thinking squares.

A student is surprised by the transparent wings of the glasswing butterfly. She marks her thinking with a sketch on a sticky note.

DAY 18 Guided Practice

Focused Instruction

When you meet with your partners to discuss your nonfiction book, you will start with the title of the book, what it is about, and your opinion of it. Did you like the book? Why or why not? Here are some nonfiction books I have read to you. I will read the title and then we will say what the book is about and discuss our opinions.

Independent Practice

Everyone gets two thinking squares for today. Remember to use sketches to remind yourself of your thinking on each page.

- Students read independently for 10 minutes.

Tell your partner the title and your opinion of the book. Take a minute to think about what you will say. Now meet with your partners to discuss your books.

- Record the ways students are talking about their books. Share this language in the Wrap-Up.

Wrap-Up

I want to share with you the ways I heard you talking about your books with your partners today.

DAY 19 Commitment

Focused Instruction

We talk with friends about nonfiction because we are reading about topics that interest us. Can you think about the kinds of nonfiction books you want to read this year? Let us chart our ideas for nonfiction books we will read during the year that are about the things we love and would like to know more about.

Independent Practice

Today we will spend our independent reading time in our school library. Our librarian will show us where the nonfiction area of the library is located. You will each get to choose one nonfiction book that reflects your interest. I will check out the books and add them to your tabletop baskets.

- As books are checked out, students share their choices with one another.

Wrap-Up

- Partners share their book choices with each other.

DAY 20 Commitment

Focused Instruction

We are going to celebrate how we have grown as readers during this month. We have learned a lot as nonfiction readers. What are some of the things you know about nonfiction books now that you did not know before? What can you do now as a reader that you could not do before?

- Record student responses.

Independent Practice

In independent reading time today, look through the tabletop baskets to remind yourself of all you have learned by reading nonfiction. Decide on one book that you especially liked. Put two thinking squares in the book where you would like to talk about your thinking. You will get a chance to share your book and your thinking at the Wrap-Up session.

Wrap-Up

- Each child shares one aspect of the nonfiction book he or she liked in small groups of three or four. Students use the same book-talk language they practiced throughout this unit.
- Show students where nonfiction books are kept in the classroom or school library.

Writing About Our Lives

The worlds our children live in hover somewhere between reality and dreams. We do not want to disrupt that time in our children's lives. They are as fascinated by the magic of reality as they are by the very real possibility of magic. We can embrace that in this unit by giving our students the opportunity to write about topics that are real but touched by magic: writing about learning how to kick a soccer ball, the fur on a dog, how to bake a cake with mom or dad. These things are all magical at this age. Never think nonfiction is in any way about taking that away.

Knowing and Sharing: Nonfiction Writing

GENRE

Why Teach This?

- To expose students to writing nonfiction.
- To learn how writers inform others through writing.
- To teach students how nonfiction authors find their writing ideas.
- To teach students how to incorporate nonfiction text features into their writing.
- To introduce students to the concept of research.

Framing Questions

- How do I write nonfiction?
- What does nonfiction writing look like and sound like?

Unit Goals

- Students will write facts about a topic of choice.
- Students will use nonfiction text features to convey information about a topic.
- Students will gather additional information about a self-selected topic through research.
- Students will use conventional spelling for one content-specific word in their writing.

Anchor Texts

- *Apples* by Gilda Berger and Melvin Berger
- *Busy as a Bee* by Melvin Berger
- *Chameleons Are Cool* by Martin Jenkins
- *Chameleon's Colors* by Chisato Tashiro
- *Dogs* by Gail Gibbons
- *Fire! Fire!* by Gail Gibbons
- *Garden Friends* by DK Publishing
- *Harry the Dirty Dog* by Gene Zion
- *I Love Tennis* by DK Publishing
- *Leaves* by Gilda and Melvin Berger
- *Meet the Dinosaurs* by DK Publishing
- *Rules Help* by Marvin Buckley
- *The Ultimate Playground and Recess Game Book* by Guy Bailey

Resource Sheets

- Paper Samples (Resources 5.2–5.5)

Unit Assessment Knowing and Sharing: Nonfiction Writing			GENRE
Student name:	EMERGING	DEVELOPING	INDEPENDENT
Writes informational text.			
Uses nonfiction text features effectively in writing.			
Finds additional information about a topic by researching.			
Writes an introduction for a nonfiction book.			
Edits the spelling of a content-specific word.			

Stage of the Unit	Focused Instruction You will	Independent Practice Students will
IMMERSION 3 days	• read *Chameleons Are Cool* and discuss the passion nonfiction authors often have for their topic. • read *Chameleon's Colors* and explore differences between writing facts and writing a story. • notice how nonfiction books look different from fiction books.	• make a list of things they are passionate about. • write or draw factual information about one of the passions on their list. • make their own work look like nonfiction.
IDENTIFICATION 1 day	• identify how nonfiction writing looks and sounds different from fiction; create a list of how nonfiction looks and sounds.	• write and draw information about a passion so that it looks and sounds like nonfiction.
GUIDED PRACTICE 11 days	• use *Dogs*, *Apples*, and *Leaves* to discuss how nonfiction authors choose their topic, gather information, and organize it in a book; begin writing a nonfiction book about recess. • Read *I Love Tennis*; discuss how authors choose topics that interest them; create a list of topics that interest students. • demonstrate using the sound strategy to carefully spell words.	• write facts about a topic of choice. • write multiple facts on one topic, one per page. • use the sound strategy as one way to spell tricky words in their writing.

GUIDED PRACTICE (continued)	• use *Dogs* and *Harry the Dirty Dog* to compare the illustrations in nonfiction versus fiction books. • read *Garden Friends* and discuss how and why nonfiction writers use diagrams in their writing. • read *Busy as a Bee*; discuss how nonfiction authors conduct research. • discuss the importance of research; begin a chart of questions to ask the expert on recess. • read *The Ultimate Playground and Recess Game Book* and demonstrate how other books can be used as a way to research a topic. • notice how nonfiction authors introduce a topic on the first page; use *Garden Friends* and *Meet the Dinosaurs*. • study the titles of anchor texts; vote on a title for class book. • demonstrate spelling a content-specific word conventionally by looking through other books on the same topic.	• draw realistic and detailed illustrations to go with their writing. • make a diagram that refers to one aspect of their topics. • conduct research to add additional information to their writing. • choose one topic to make into a book and write an introduction page. • write a title for their book that sounds like a nonfiction title. • spell one content-specific word in their book conventionally.
COMMITMENT 1 day	• guide students through a reflection: "How have I grown as a writer? What do I know about writing nonfiction books?"	• reflect about their learning in this unit with a partner; read their nonfiction book to an audience.
TOTAL: 16 DAYS		

Getting Started

During the Focused Instruction, you will demonstrate nonfiction writing through the creation of a class book. We suggest that you decide on the topic for your book ahead of time. It is helpful to choose a familiar topic, so students can focus on the process of the writing. You may also consider choosing a topic that you are currently studying in science or social studies, incorporating into writing time what students are learning in a content area.

Structures and Routines

Partnerships

Students meet with partners at the beginning of Independent Practice time to orally rehearse their ideas that will be written and sketched that day. We use what we know about the students' interests to form partnerships, if possible.

Teaching Materials

When selecting anchor texts, we consider the following teaching opportunities within them: where the author got the idea for the book, nonfiction text features, and all the ways the author conveys information. We use different anchor texts to illustrate different teaching points.

Topic Choice

- *Chameleons Are Cool* by Martin Jenkins
- *Dogs* by Gail Gibbons
- *I Love Tennis* by DK Publishing

Text Features

- *Busy as a Bee* by Melvin Berger
- *Dogs* by Gail Gibbons
- *Garden Friends* by DK Readers

Ways Authors Convey Information

- *Meet the Dinosaurs* by DK Readers
- *Pumpkins, Apples, Leaves, Seed to Plant, Bees, Polar Bears Live on Ice* (all from the Scholastic Time-to-Discover series)
- *Rules Help* by Marvin Buckley

Texts That Support the Class Nonfiction Book

- *Hopscotch, Hangman, Hot Potato and Ha Ha Ha* by Jack Maguire
- *The Ultimate Playground and Recess Game Book* by Guy Bailey

Student Materials

Paper

Students write on paper that has a picture box and four lines for writing (see Resource 5.4). Some of your students may want space to write even more information on a page, so you may want to create paper with additional lines as well.

Stages of the Unit

Immersion

In this stage of the unit, students are immersed in nonfiction writing—identifying the writing as factual and identifying the unique look of nonfiction books. This Immersion period begins as students start reading nonfiction books in reading time and continues for two days during writing time.

Identification

The look, sound, and purpose of nonfiction texts are articulated in this stage. Identifying the characteristics of nonfiction text is addressed in the reading unit.

Guided Practice

Students write informational books on topics they know a lot about. Topics may come from their interests, passions, and life experiences. Many children have pets—dogs, cats, fish, and hamsters could all be topics for a book. Other topics include interests such as soccer, baking, dress-up, and so on. In this stage, students learn how to plan out their ideas on graphic organizers and then use them to write their book.

Commitment

Students reflect on the process they went through finding ideas that matter and how to incorporate text features that enhance the subject matter.

Day-by-Day Lessons

DAY 1 Immersion

Focused Instruction

We have been reading a lot of nonfiction books. Nonfiction writers have passions about things and love to find out about them. I am going to read aloud to you from a book called Chameleons Are Cool *by Martin Jenkins. Martin loves chameleons. Let's listen to how much he loves his topic. Can you hear it? What are you passionate about? Some of these are going to become great topic ideas for our own nonfiction writing.*

Independent Practice

Today you will talk to your partners about things you love. These may become topics for books you will write. After you talk with your partner you will list some of your passions on list paper.

Name John

My Passions

socr

DOGS

inscts

A student draws and labels his passions.

Wrap-Up

- Several students share the topics they are passionate about.

What are some passions and interests we have as a class? Let's make a list of the things we are passionate about as a class.

DAY 2 Immersion

Focused Instruction

We are thinking about how fiction is different from nonfiction. Here is another book about chameleons called Chameleon's Colors *by Chisato Tashiro. Let me read this one to you. I notice right away that this one sounds really different. That is because* Chameleon's Colors *is a fiction book. One way that we can tell these books are different is that Martin's book had information, or facts, in it to teach you. Nonfiction writers include facts in their books to teach their reader something new. Today I am going to choose one of the topics off our class list and write or draw a fact about it.*

- Model drawing or writing a fact from the class list.

Independent Practice

Today in your writing, choose one of the topics you are passionate about and write or draw a fact about it. A fact is something that teaches us about a topic. We can call these "teaching pictures" or "teaching words."

Wrap-Up

- Select two students to share: one who created teaching pictures and one who created teaching words.

DAY 3 Immersion

Focused Instruction

We have read a nonfiction and fiction book about chameleons. There were things you learned about how nonfiction books look different from fiction books. Let's review what you learned. Now let's think about how you can make your writing look like the nonfiction books you are reading. I will reread the fact we wrote yesterday. I will think about what I can add to it to make it look like a page in a nonfiction book. Now it is your turn. Think about the fact you wrote during writing time yesterday. Now think about what you can add to your paper to make it look like a page from a nonfiction book and tell your partner what you can add to make it look like a page from a nonfiction book.

Independent Practice

When you have finished adding to your paper from yesterday, you can go on to a new piece of paper. You can sketch or write another fact about the same topic or go onto another passion from your list.

Wrap-Up

- Have two students share how they revised their work to make it look like a page from a nonfiction book.

DAY 4 Identification

Focused Instruction

You have been reading nonfiction books and paying attention to the way they sound and look. Today we are going to list what we have noticed about the way nonfiction books sound and look.

- Revisit the chart you created during reading time or make a new one with students here.

Independent Practice

What passion will you write about today? Choose a topic from your list and tell your partner what you will sketch and write.

Wrap-Up

- Choose a topic from the class list of passions and create a sketch and write a fact about it.

DAY 5 Guided Practice

Focused Instruction

Today we are going to think about how nonfiction authors learned information about a topic in order to write a book about it. This will help you think about what you might write a nonfiction book about. I am going to think about where Gail Gibbons got the idea to write her book Dogs.

Gail Gibbons wrote this book, which is all about dogs. I am wondering if she got the idea to write this book because she has a pet dog. If she has a dog at her house, she would know a lot about that animal from living with it each day. Or maybe she does not have a dog of her own but loves them and knows many people who have dogs. She must really like these animals if she wrote a whole book about them.

Together we are going to write a nonfiction class book. I know we love recess so I am going to show you how together we can write a nonfiction book about it. It is something we all know a lot about, and it is something we like to do. Those are good qualities for a nonfiction topic. What do you think Gail Gibbons did to get ready to write her book about dogs? Let's brainstorm some ideas. (Possible responses: she watched her dog, she asked her friends questions, she sketched dogs, she went for a walk to see dogs.) *We are going to do some of those same things when we write our recess book.*

We are going to really pay attention to what we do at recess, and we are going to write all that down. Let's begin. Turn to your partner and share one thing you do at recess. (Partners share with each other.) The thing you shared is a fact! We will be writing a nonfiction class book about recess. Let's gather facts about this topic. Later today when you are at recess, be careful observers of all that goes on.

Independent Practice

During Independent Practice, I want you to think about a topic you care about and try writing some facts about it. Choose something you love, like recess. Share with your partner what you will write about today and then begin.

Wrap-Up

Let us notice how Melvin and Gilda Berger organize facts about a topic in a book. (Read Apples *and* Leaves.) *Notice the text layout of one fact per page. So many of you know lots of facts about your passions. You may want to organize a book about your passion by writing one fact on each page like* Apples *and* Leaves.

DAY 6 Guided Practice

Focused Instruction

- Read *I Love Tennis*. Discuss the idea that writers write about topics that interest them. Ask students to talk about their own interests with their classmates.

Independent Practice

Share with your partner your writing plan for today. What topic will you write about and what is the fact you will write? What are your plans to make the page look like nonfiction? After you are finished sharing your plans with your partner, you can get started.

Wrap-Up

- Add to the chart of student passions.

DAY 7 Guided Practice

Focused Instruction

- Have students come to the meeting area with dry-erase boards and markers for this lesson.

Today we are going to practice being strong spellers using one of the strategies we studied earlier in the year—the sound strategy. I will use this strategy to write another fact for our recess book. I want to write the fact that recess is twenty minutes long. I want to write the word "jump." I am going to use the sound strategy to write as many letters as I can. Let us all try to write the word "jump" on our boards.

- Engage students in practicing spelling three different words for the class nonfiction book.

Independent Practice

Today use your sound spelling strategies to help you through the tricky words you want to write.

Wrap-Up

- Share some of the words students used in their writing from Independent Practice.

DAY 8 Guided Practice

Focused Instruction

Dogs *by Gail Gibbons is a nonfiction book with illustrations. We are going to compare these illustrations with the ones in* Harry the Dirty Dog *by Gene Zion.*

- If necessary, guide students to notice that the illustrations in *Dogs* are realistic and detailed compared to the ones in *Harry the Dirty Dog*.

Independent Practice

You have learned that the illustrations in nonfiction are realistic and detailed. In your writing today, please write at least one fact and draw one realistic and detailed picture for your topic.

Wrap-Up

- Choose a few students' work to share and discuss.

DAY 9 Guided Practice

Focused Instruction

You noticed that some nonfiction books have diagrams. Our book Garden Friends *has one on each page. Let us look at one of them now. Think about what kind of diagram we could add to our recess book.*

- Discuss and then add a labeled diagram to the class book.

Independent Practice

Think about the topics you have written about so far. What kind of diagram could you make for one of the topics? What words would you use to label your diagram? Share your thinking with your partner and then begin.

Wrap-Up

- Share some student diagrams.

A kindergartener makes a diagram of a football player. He labels the drawing with the words: *helmet*, *shoulder pads*, *cleats*, *gloves*. His accompanying fact reads, "Football players wear a lot of equipment."

DAY 10 Guided Practice

Focused Instruction

• Read aloud Melvin Berger's book *Busy as a Bee*.

In this book, Melvin Berger shows how much he knows about bees. He tells us what he knows. Nonfiction writers do something called "research" to add facts to their books. Research is when a writer finds more information about a topic. Talk to the person next to you about how you think Melvin Berger could have researched or found information for his book. Let's chart all the ways he might have researched his topic (talking to people, observing his world, and so on).

Independent Practice

Think of a topic you have already written about. How could you do research to find out more information about it? Think of a person or perhaps a book or a place you could go that would give you more information about your topic. Talk to your partner about your topic and your research.

• Students start planning how to conduct research for one of their topics. Students then continue to write and draw about one of their chosen topics.

Wrap-Up

• Choose students to share their research plan.

What are the ways we can add more information to our recess book? Is there anyone who knows about recess whom we can talk to? Who can we talk to who is an "expert" on recess? (Perhaps your students will select the principal or an older student.)

DAY 11 Guided Practice

Focused Instruction

Tomorrow we will invite our recess expert in and ask him or her questions about recess to learn more about our topic. Today, let's brainstorm questions we can ask to prepare ourselves.

• Chart questions.

Asking our expert these questions is how we will conduct our research. The new information we learn will be added to our book to teach others even more about recess!

Independent Practice

I am going to give you an index card, and on that card I want you to think of one question to ask someone about your topic: maybe it is your mom, if you are writing your book about something you do at home. Maybe it is a friend in this class. You can continue adding to your nonfiction books after writing your question.

Wrap-Up

• Share student questions. Share student writing that exemplifies what you want other students to do with their nonfiction books.

DAY 12 Guided Practice

Focused Instruction

One way to get more information for your nonfiction book is by talking to someone who knows a lot about your topic. Another way to do research for your book is by reading other books. Let's look at these books: The Ultimate Playground and Recess Game Book *by Guy Bailey and* Hopscotch, Hangman, Hot Potato, and Ha Ha Ha *by Jack Maguire. These are both nonfiction books we can look at to help us in our research. Let's look at the table of contents in these books to see what we can learn. We learn about games people play at recess. We can make a page in our class book that will include our research. We can add a page that describes the games children play at recess in our school. You may not need to use other books to research your topic, but it is another way nonfiction writers find out more.*

- Model adding a page in the class book using research from another nonfiction book.

Independent Practice

You will add more information about one of the topics you have written about. Ask a friend or an expert about something related to your topic, use your own experiences, or find a book that relates to your topic as a way to add more.

Wrap-Up

Who used a book to find more information about their topic? What was the book and what information did you find in it?

- Call on a few students who are conducting research to find additional facts. If others are having difficulty finding additional information for their books, they can ask the class for suggestions at this time.

A student researches frogs by talking with her mom. The research information was added in the second sentence: *Frogs are amphibians.*

DAY 13 Guided Practice

Focused Instruction

Today we are going to study how authors begin their nonfiction books. Let's look at the first page of Garden Friends *and* Meet the Dinosaur. *Notice how the authors introduce their topic on the first page. Now let's add a page to our recess book that introduces readers to the topic. What should we write on this page? Tell the person next to you what you think we should write on this page.*

- Add a first page to the recess book based on student thinking.

Thar are 'ts all
Difmnt kinz uV insets
in the wrlD.

A student writes an introduction page for her insect book: "There are lots of different kinds of insects in the world."

Independent Practice

Today I want you to choose one topic that you have been writing a lot about. The topic you choose should be the one you are most excited about and the one with the best facts and drawings. Today, you'll gather all the facts and drawings you have made about that topic and you will make it a book. What will you write on the first page to introduce readers to your topic? Discuss your writing plan with your partner, and then you may begin.

Wrap-Up

Listen to how your classmates have introduced readers to their books on the first page.

- Read examples of student writing.

DAY 14 Guided Practice

Focused Instruction

Let's reread the nonfiction recess book we are writing. Rereading is a great thing to do to see if we are missing any parts or if it sounds just how we want it to sound. Also, it helps us get the big idea about our book so we can think of a title.

- Read the class book.

Let's look at some of the titles of the nonfiction books we have read together. The Ultimate Playground and Recess Game Book *and* Chameleons Are Cool. *What feels good about these titles? What are the qualities they share?* (They are direct, explanatory, fun and amusing, catchy for the reader, and so on.) *Now we are going to make a list of possible titles for our book. Tomorrow, after we have all had time to think about the choices, we will vote for our book title.*

Independent Practice

Write a few possible titles for your book. Then share your ideas with your partner to see what your partner thinks. In the end, the title is your decision because you are the author.

Wrap-Up

Reread the possible titles you have written for your book and make a star next to the one you like best. Now we will go around and everyone will read their book title.

DAY 15 Guided Practice

Focused Instruction

Today we are going to be looking at the spelling of the words in our books. You have done a very good job of using your sound and sight strategies to spell words in your book so far. Now we are going to think about a word in your book for which it would be important to have the dictionary spelling. Let's choose one word from our recess book: "playground." Let's make sure we have the dictionary spelling of this word since it is so important to the big idea in our book. Where can I find that word? I know it is in the title of our book, The Ultimate Playground and Recess Game Book. *I can copy the word from the cover of that book. Now we will look carefully through our book to find other times we have used the word so we can correct it. This is called editing. Grown-up writers do this all the time! Think about a word in your book that feels important. Where do you think you could find the dictionary spelling for that word?* (Another book, a basic dictionary, the word wall, and so on.) *What word in your book will be the important one for which you will want to have the dictionary spelling? Turn to your partner and share the word that should be spelled correctly in your book.*

Independent Practice

Now I would like you to read your nonfiction book again. Once you have decided on your word, you will try to find the spelling of it and write it on a sticky note. If you are unable to find your word in a book, try spelling it again on your sticky note using your sound or sight spelling strategy. I will make sure you have the dictionary spelling of the word for tomorrow and write it on your sticky note.

Wrap-Up

- Students share the word they found the dictionary spelling for and where they found it.

DAY 16 Commitment

Focused Instruction

We are finishing our study of nonfiction writing. Today we are going to take the time to reflect on what we have learned in this unit. What have you learned about nonfiction writing? How is nonfiction writing different from story writing? Share with your neighbor one new thing you have learned as a writer during this unit. What was the most difficult part of the unit? Share with your neighbor. What about your writing and learning from this unit makes you the most proud? Share this with your neighbor also.

- Listen in and record students' reflections.

Wrap-Up

We are going to celebrate this unit by reading our books to our buddies, parents, and/or friends.

Punctuation Power

How fitting to come into the ending season, and to cap off a nonfiction writing unit with a unit on ending punctuation! Your kindergarteners absolutely adore punctuation: their fascination for the ellipsis knows no bounds, and oh, what they can do with an exclamation point! This work should feel marked by the ongoing delight of discovery—of students' understanding and bold use of conventions.

We were working with a kindergartener named Alianna, and she had placed a gigantic, round black period, carefully filled in, after every single word. We could see it had taken her much time to do this task, so we complimented her profusely and she just beamed at us. We said, "Alianna, it looks like you love periods! Can we show you when to put them at the end of sentences?" And she looked at us, with her serious, earnest eyes, and said, "I know exactly where periods go, but I just *love* them so much I put them everywhere!" Here, then, is the essence of the kindergartener: embracing everything, even something as small as a period! She loves ellipses, commas, semicolons, all the curlicues of the language itself. She is savoring the mysteries of language and playing inside them.

Reading With Expression: Using Punctuation to Enhance Fluency

CONVENTIONS

Why Teach This?

- To help students become aware of punctuation as a key to fluency.
- To teach students to read with expression.
- To illuminate the story element of character as a key component to reading narrative texts.

Framing Questions

- How can we improve our reading by paying attention to punctuation and phrasing?
- How can we get inside the lives of characters we read about by reading with expression?

Unit Goals

- Students will use punctuation and picture clues to inform their reading aloud.
- Students will adjust their voices to create different characters as they read aloud.
- Students will read with expression.
- Students will recognize dialogue marks and other indicators for when a character speaks.

Anchor Texts

- *Daniel's Pet* by Alma Flor Ada
- *Green Eggs and Ham* by Dr. Seuss
- *Mrs. Wishy Washy* by Joy Cowley
- *A Splendid Friend Indeed* by Suzanne Bloom
- *There Is a Bird on Your Head* by Mo Willems

Unit Assessment Reading With Expression: Using Punctuation to Enhance Fluency			CONVENTIONS
Student name:	EMERGING	DEVELOPING	INDEPENDENT
Identifies characters in a story.			
Uses punctuation to read with expression.			
Uses picture clues to read with expression.			
Distinguishes between characters by reading with expression.			

Stage of the Unit	Focused Instruction You will	Independent Practice Students will
IMMERSION 1 day	• read aloud from *Green Eggs and Ham* and demonstrate how readers read with expression, using picture clues and punctuation to guide their voices; ask students what they noticed about your voice during the read-aloud.	• read books with partners, choosing texts to read aloud to one another with expression; take turns reading aloud, switching off for each page.
IDENTIFICATION 3 days	• use *Mrs. Wishy Washy* and identify two clues readers look for to guide their reading expression, punctuation and picture clues; model using each clue to guide your vocal quality. • read *There Is a Bird on Your Head*, using character voices; ask students what they notice about how you change your voice for each character. • read *Daniel's Pet*; identify the dialogue marks in a fiction text and show students how to identify when different characters are speaking.	• read aloud with partners, using punctuation and picture clues to guide their vocal expression. • identify dialogue marks in a fiction text to determine when different characters are speaking.

| GUIDED PRACTICE
3 days | • read *Green Eggs and Ham*; use character voices for Sam and the Cat in the Hat; ask students to share voices they would use for these characters.

• read *A Splendid Friend Indeed*; use character voices; ask students to share voices they would use for the characters in the book. | • read aloud with partners, using different voices for each character; take turns being different characters in books. |
| COMMITMENT
2 days | • model drawing a picture of a character you love doing a special voice for; share with a partner the voice you use for the character and explain why you love that voice. | • draw a picture of a character they love doing a special voice for; share their special voices and pictures with a partner. |

TOTAL: 9 DAYS

Writing With Expression: Using Ending Punctuation to Enhance Meaning

CONVENTIONS

Why Teach This?

- To teach students proper and effective use of periods, question marks, and exclamation points.
- To demonstrate how punctuation guides a reader's reading.

Framing Question

- Why do writers use punctuation?
- How does punctuation influence the sound of our words?

Unit Goals

- Students will demonstrate proper use of periods.
- Students will demonstrate proper use of question marks.
- Students will demonstrate proper use of exclamation marks.
- Students will explain why writers use punctuation in their writing.

Anchor Texts

- *Daniel's Pet* by Alma Flor Ada
- *David Goes to School* by David Shannon
- *I Love My New Toy* by Mo Willems
- *Shortcut* by Donald Crews

Unit Assessment Writing With Expression: Using Ending Punctuation to Enhance Meaning			CONVENTIONS
Student name:	EMERGING	DEVELOPING	INDEPENDENT
Uses periods at the end of sentences.			
Uses question marks at the end of question sentences.			
Uses exclamation points at the end of exciting, thrilling, "yelling" sentences.			
Can explain why writers use punctuation.			

Stage of the Unit	**Focused Instruction** You will	**Independent Practice** Students will
IMMERSION 1 day	• on a chart, show students a passage from *Shortcuts* that contains a lot of punctuation (periods, question marks, exclamation points); read aloud, pointing as you read and using your voice to illustrate how the punctuation guides your reading; ask students what they notice about your reading and why you	• revisit a past piece of writing and reread it with an attention to the ending punctuation—or lack of punctuation—and then revise the punctuation where necessary.

IMMERSION (continued)	changed your voice for different sentences in the story; emphasize that punctuation helps readers understand how to read a story (read the passage again without punctuation and ask students to notice the difference).	
IDENTIFICATION 1 day	• read I Love My New Toy! and create a chart that identifies different kinds of ending punctuation and explores why a writer uses each.	• write with an attention to ending punctuation.
GUIDED PRACTICE 3 days	• read Daniel's Pet and show students various sentences with periods; demonstrate when periods are used (at the end of sentences) and read some sentences without periods to show their importance. • read David Goes to School and show students a variety of sentences with question marks. Demonstrate when the question marks are used (at the end of a question sentence) and read some sentences without question marks to show their importance in the writing. • reread parts of anchor texts and show students various sentences with exclamation marks. Demonstrate when the exclamation marks are used (at the end of exciting, thrilling, yelling sentences) and read some sentences without exclamation marks to show their importance in the writing.	• use periods at the end of sentences in their writing (students may write in a genre of their choice). • use periods or question marks at the end of sentences in their writing, depending on the sentence. • use periods, question marks, or exclamation marks at the end of sentences in their writing, depending on the sentence (students may choose to continue their short story or start a new one).
COMMITMENT 1 day	• reflect on the improvement in the punctuation of student writing; name specific students and share examples.	• share their punctuated writing with a friend; write one of their punctuated sentences on a sentence strip (strips are hung around the writing center as guides for students to refer to during writing).
TOTAL: 6 DAYS		

Happy Endings

Kindergarteners love happy endings, so it is no surprise they love fictional stories, where things can work out just right, in spite of problems. Fictional characters so brilliantly rendered by our greatest children's book authors are not simplistic; they are deeply human, even when they are in animal form. Frog and Toad, Olivia, Owen, Little Bear, Frances, and Sylvester all inhabit the consciousness of our developing readers because they come alive in all their imperfect yet completely entrancing ways. And happiness is always possible.

Connecting to Story Elements: Reading Fiction

STRATEGY

Why Teach This?

- To show students that making connections in reading deepens understanding.
- To familiarize students with the characteristics of the fiction genre.
- To introduce students to a variety of fictional characters.
- To introduce students to the predictable pattern of problem and solution.
- To show students how authors indicate the passage of time in their stories.

Framing Questions

- How can we identify the qualities of fiction?
- How can we deepen our understanding of story elements?

Unit Goals

- Students will read in leveled books.
- Students will identify the characteristics of fiction.
- Students will make baskets of books that show different ways of depicting the passage of time.
- Students will discuss different character relationships in fiction.
- Students will identify the problem and solution.

Anchor Texts

- *Hey, Al!* by Arthur Yorinks
- *Little Gorilla* by Ruth Bernstein
- *Max and Ruby* by Rosemary Wells
- *Olivia Saves the Circus* by Ian Falconer
- *Owen* by Kevin Henkes
- *The Paper Bag Princess* by Robert Munsch
- *Ruby's Rainy Day* by Rosemary Wells
- *Sylvester and the Magic Pebble* by William Steig

Unit Assessment Connecting to Story Elements: Reading Fiction			STRATEGY
Student name:	EMERGING	DEVELOPING	INDEPENDENT
Categorizes fiction from nonfiction.			
Describes relationships between characters.			
Identifies differences in uses of time in simple text.			
Describes a problem and solution in story.			

Stage of the Unit	Focused Instruction You will	Independent Practice Students will
IMMERSION 4 days	• discuss with students their understanding of fictional stories. • revisit *Olivia Saves the Circus* and *Sylvester and the Magic Pebble*; identify and reflect on various fiction characters (people, animals, toys, and so on). • read *Hey, Al!* and *The Paper Bag Princess* and notice how authors show setting. • read *Ruby's Rainy Day* and notice how authors show the passage of time.	• browse familiar fiction books, exploring the characteristics of fiction writing. • browse familiar fiction books, noticing the types of characters in fictional stories (people, animals, toys, and so on). • browse familiar picture books, noticing various settings in fiction stories (real or imagined). • browse familiar picture books, searching for clues that indicate the passage of time.
IDENTIFICATION 1 day	• list the qualities of fiction stories. • name what we have learned about time passing in stories.	• read independently and with partners.

GUIDED PRACTICE 8 days (two days of instruction for each bullet point)	• talk about relationships between characters in the books *Max and Ruby*, *Owen*, and *Little Gorilla*. • model how an author depicts the passage of time in *Sylvester and the Magic Pebble* (years), *Olivia Saves the Circus* (one day) and *Ruby's Rainy Day* (minutes). • study the problem and solution in *Hey, Al!* • reread one of the anchor texts and demonstrate retelling a familiar book that includes an understanding of character relationships, passage of time, and problem and solution.	• discuss with partners the relationships between characters in one of their independent reading books (a leveled book or familiar picture book). • discuss with partners how much time passes in one of their books; show evidence from the pictures in their books that indicate the passage of time. • mark the problem in a story with a "P" on a sticky note and the solution with an "S." • retell a familiar book with a partner, including statements about the relationship between characters, the passage of time, and the problem and solution.
COMMITMENT 1 day	• reflect on the growth you have witnessed in the students.	• choose a favorite book from this unit to dramatize, paint a favorite part, or build the setting with blocks.
TOTAL: 14 DAYS		

EARLY FALL

LATE FALL

WINTER

SPRING

Affirm the Power of Story

We notice kindergarteners write pages and pages when creating imaginary stories. Let's never underestimate the sheer value of quantity (of words and pages!) to the kindergarten child as she becomes more fluent with print. The more she writes, the better she will get. Additionally, we are honing her understanding of story elements and the affirming the power of story. So let's include imaginative stories in our curriculum.

Connecting to Imagination: Writing Fiction

GENRE

Why Teach This?

- To familiarize students with the characteristics of the fiction genre.
- To develop students' understanding of story elements and sequence.
- To teach students idea-generating strategies.

Framing Questions

- What is fiction writing?
- How do writers write fiction?
- How do writers find their ideas for fiction stories?

Unit Goals

- Students will identify the characteristics of fiction writing.
- Students will generate story ideas independently.
- Students will write fiction stories with a clear beginning, middle, and end.
- Students will write fiction stories with a problem and solution.
- Students will write fiction stories with detailed, informative illustrations.
- Students will write fiction stories with a strong lead and ending.
- Students will pay attention to the passage of time in their stories.

Anchor Texts

- *Abuela* by Arthur Dorros
- *Hey, Al!* by Arthur Yorinks
- *Little Gorilla* by Ruth Bernstein
- *The Little Engine That Could* by Watty Piper
- *The Paper Bag Princess* by Robert Munsch
- *Ruby's Rainy Day* by Rosemary Wells
- *A Snowy Surprise* by Amy Hest
- *Super Hero* by Marc Tauss
- *Sylvester and the Magic Pebble* by William Steig
- *The Trip* by Ezra Jack Keats

Unit Assessment Connecting to Imagination: Writing Fiction			GENRE
Student name:	EMERGING	DEVELOPING	INDEPENDENT
Writes and draws stories that are sequential.			
Generates story ideas independently.			
Stretches stories across three pages or more (beginning, middle, and end).			
Writes stories with a problem and solution.			
Plays with conveying the passage of time in writing and illustrations.			
Writes stories with a strong lead.			
Writes stories with a strong ending.			

Stage of the Unit	Focused Instruction You will	Independent Practice Students will
IMMERSION 1 day	• use *Little Gorilla* and reflect on the characteristics of fiction writing, identifying how a fiction book is different from other books; model writing a short fiction story inspired by the anchor text.	• write a short fiction story inspired by the anchor text.
IDENTIFICATION 2 days	• read *The Trip* and discuss qualities of fiction stories (which of the story elements are clearly fictional?); use favorite anchor texts to identify how writers include all story ingredients in their stories. • read *The Little Engine That Could* and discuss how writers may have found their story ideas (their imagination, inspired by another book or by a real-life event).	• write a short fiction story that may be inspired by a favorite fiction story. • work with partners to hypothesize how authors of anchor texts got their story ideas.
GUIDED PRACTICE 10 days	• read *Abuela* and discuss how fiction writers use their imagination to find their story ideas. • model generating story ideas from thinking about a character (pirate stories, princess stories, animal stories, and so on).	• use their imagination and anchor texts to find and write fiction story ideas. • find a story idea by deciding on a fictional character on which to base their story. • discuss with partners their story ideas (which include a problem and solution) before writing on paper.

GUIDED PRACTICE *(continued)*	• discuss how writers usually incorporate a problem and solution in their story; read *Shy Charles* and identify the problem and solution in the story. • model generating a story idea by thinking of a problem and then a solution; use *Super Hero* and *Sylvester and the Magic Pebble* to demonstrate a story that includes magic or a superhero as the solution to a problem. • demonstrate how to use a Story String to develop, organize, and rehearse a story idea. • read *A Snowy Surprise* and demonstrate how writers sequence their stories in order; model how to take a story and stretch it across three pages or more (beginning, middle, and end). • use *The Paper Bag Princess* to model finding a story idea by thinking of a fictional setting; demonstrate planning it across three pages. • read *Ruby's Rainy Day* and model how an author considers the passage of time when writing a story by adding time words and/or illustrations to show time passing. • model writing a strong lead, or opening sentence, for your story; reread your first sentence and revise it so it hooks the reader; reread *A Snowy Surprise* and discuss the first line. • reread *Super Hero* and *The Paper Bag Princess* to study tie-ups (endings) in stories; model rereading the ending of a story you have written and revise it (by adding more or using story language).	• generate a story idea by deciding on a problem then the solution to the problem. • use a Story String to rehearse their story ideas with a partner before writing on paper. • decide on a story idea and plan it with a Story String and partner before writing on paper. • use three-page books when writing new fiction stories. • generate a story idea by thinking of fictional settings. • revise one story by adding illustrations or adding time words to show passage of time ("later that night," "the next day," "a couple of days later"). • reread the first sentences of their stories; revise them so they hook the reader. • reread the ending of their stories and revise the ending of one.
COMMITMENT 2 days	• choose a story that you have written during this unit to finish and publish; model going through and looking for things to add, clean up, or clarify. • meet with a partner (a teacher or another adult) to share your story; read it to your partner and share the illustrations.	• choose a story they have written to finish and publish; go through and edit the spelling of three words, capital letters, periods. • meet with a partner to share their stories.
TOTAL: 15 DAYS		

Forward Thinking

Summer is around the corner. The windows are open and the breezes pour in, or if you live in the southern part of our country, your windows are tightly shut and you can nearly see frost on your breath from the chill of the air conditioners! Your young ones are dreaming of their long summer days. You too are thinking ahead—planning your summer beach read, or making plans for summer work. While our minds wander in those directions, let us create units that celebrate the forward-thinking mind, and help our children make summer plans that include reading and writing. Armed with a special summer writing notebook and a plan for books they will read and browse, they leave your room with all your countless gifts to them—never to be forgotten. So, too, are their gifts to us.

Looking Back, Looking Forward: Making Summer Reading Plans

PROCESS

Why Teach This?
- To reflect on the reading work done over the school year.
- To make plans for summer reading.

Framing Questions
- How did your reading grow and change during this school year?
- What are some reading goals you have for the summer?

Unit Goals
- Students will reflect on themselves as readers: favorite books, favorite reading spots, favorite units, what felt hard, what felt good.
- Students will make a "Reading Reflections" book to document some of their reading experiences in kindergarten.
- Students will make plans for summer reading.

Anchor Text
- *My Kindergarten* by Rosemary Wells

Resource Sheets
- Reading Reflection Book (Resources 5.6)

Unit Assessment Looking Back, Looking Forward: Making Summer Reading Plans			PROCESS
Student name:	EMERGING	DEVELOPING	INDEPENDENT
Identifies qualities of a reader in self.			
Identifies some favorite books, authors, and/or units of study.			
Identifies how his or her reading life has changed since the beginning of kindergarten.			
Makes plans for summer reading.			

Looking Back...

Stage of the Unit	Focused Instruction You will	Independent Practice Students will
IMMERSION 1 day	• review the meaning of the word "reflection" and explain how we are going to think back on our year as readers. • model thinking aloud about some of your favorite read-alouds and favorite reading units and activities.	• work with a partner and talk about at least one favorite read-aloud and why it was a favorite. • work with a partner and reflect on a favorite reading unit and/or reading activity and why it was a favorite.
IDENTIFICATION 1 day	• name and identify ways we can reflect on ourselves as readers: favorite books, favorite genre, favorite activity, what you can now do as a reader, when reading felt good, when reading felt hard.	• identify a time in kindergarten when reading felt hard and a time that you felt really strong as a reader; share with a partner.
GUIDED PRACTICE 5 days	• make a list of students' favorite read-alouds from the year; share your favorite, draw a scene from the book, and record the title. • reflect on books students have read independently throughout the year that they really seemed to enjoy (leveled or nonleveled books); make a list of some favorite independent reading books. • reflect on a favorite reading unit of study from the year and discuss why it is memorable.	• discuss a favorite read-aloud with a partner, draw a picture of that book, and write the title in their reading reflections book. (See Resource 5.2.) • discuss with a partner a favorite independent reading book; draw and write the title in their reading reflections book. • discuss with a partner one unit of study that was a favorite; draw and write why the unit was a favorite in their reading reflections book.

GUIDED PRACTICE *(continued)*	• reflect on the ways students use books during play. • reflect on all that your students can do now as readers; explain what it means to be proud and how accomplishments make people feel proud.	• discuss with a partner a way they like to use books during play; draw and write the way they discussed in their reading reflections book. • discuss with a partner their reading accomplishments and which one makes them feel especially proud; draw and write about this accomplishment in their reading reflections book.
COMMITMENT 1 day	• reflect on your most favorite books, make a pile of them, and discuss how you'll be using them to start the following year.	• compile the drawings and text from the Guided Practice lessons into a book titled My Kindergarten Reading Reflections; decorate the front cover and share it with a partner.
TOTAL: 8 DAYS		

Looking Forward...

Stage of the Unit	Focused Instruction You will	Independent Practice Students will
IMMERSION 1 day	• discuss places you can read over the summer. • discuss the kinds of books you would like to read over the summer.	• work with a partner and make a list of the places they can read and the kinds of books they will choose to read over the summer.
IDENTIFICATION 1 day	• determine what things you will want in your summer reading box; chart these with the class.	• decorate the summer reading boxes in ways that will motivate and excite them as readers.
GUIDED PRACTICE 3 days	• model setting reading goals for the summer, including books you will read and where you will read them. • model keeping notes in a reading journal: writing the title, drawing and writing about one part of the book.	• decorate their summer reading journals. • draw a picture of places they can see themselves reading over the summer. • complete one page in their summer reading journals on a book of their choice.
COMMITMENT 1 day	• celebrate summer reading boxes, listing what is now in them.	• celebrate their summer reading boxes with a partner.
TOTAL: 6 DAYS		

Looking Back, Looking Forward: Making Summer Writing Plans

PROCESS

Why Teach This?

- To reflect on the writing work done over the school year.
- To make plans for summer writing.

Framing Questions

- How did your writing grow and change during the school year?
- What are some writing goals you have for the summer?

Unit Goals

- Students will reflect on themselves as writers: favorite books they wrote, favorite writing unit, struggles, and successes.
- Students will make plans for summer writing.

Materials

- Blank books to be used as Summer Writing Journals
- Portfolio of writing from the school year

Unit Assessment Looking Back, Looking Forward: Making Summer Writing Plans			PROCESS
Student name:	EMERGING	DEVELOPING	INDEPENDENT
Identifies qualities of a writer in self.			
Reflects on self as a writer: what has changed in his or her writing life since the beginning of kindergarten.			
Makes plans for summer writing.			

Looking Back...

Stage of the Unit	Focused Instruction You will	Independent Practice Students will
IMMERSION 1 day	• revisit the meaning of the word "reflection" and explain how we are going to think back on our year as writers. • model thinking aloud about some of your writing pieces from the school year.	• work with a partner and talk about at least one favorite published book. • work with a partner and reflect on a favorite writing unit and/or writing activity and why it was a favorite.
IDENTIFICATION 1 day	• identify ways you can reflect on yourself as a writer: favorite books you have written, favorite genre, favorite writing activity, what you can now do as a writer, writing successes and writing struggles. • reflect on the ways you like to play over the summer and how you may use all you know about reading and writing to enhance your play; make a class list.	• identify a time in kindergarten when writing felt like a struggle and a time when they felt really strong as a writer; share with a partner. • discuss how they may use writing in their summer activities (making a sign for a lemonade stand, writing a postcard to a relative, making a list of items to pack for a trip, making a list of items they would like from the grocery store or a wish list of summer play dates).
GUIDED PRACTICE 5 days	• model rereading a favorite piece of writing. • reflect on a writing activity from the year and discuss why it meant something to you. • discuss one of your favorite writing genres and why it was a favorite. • reflect on times writing felt hard. • discuss a time when you felt strong as a writer.	• pick a favorite published piece and share it with a partner. • discuss favorite writing topics. • discuss genres studied—fiction, nonfiction, letters, signs, and poetry—and which one meant the most to them and was their favorite to write. • reflect on what they can now do as writers. • reflect on the time when they felt strong as a writer and discuss this with a partner.
COMMITMENT 1 day	• reflect on your favorite writing activity; make a commitment to write over the summer.	• celebrate themselves as writers and share their books with a small group; make a commitment to write over the summer.
TOTAL: 8 DAYS		

Looking Forward...

Stage of the Unit	Focused Instruction You will	Independent Practice Students will
IMMERSION 1 day	• discuss places you can write over the summer. • discuss the kinds of books you'll write over the summer.	• discuss with a partner the places they can write and the kinds of writing they will do over the summer.
IDENTIFICATION 1 day	• determine what genres you may try to write over the summer.	• decorate their summer writing journals.
GUIDED PRACTICE 5 days	• model setting writing goals for the summer. • reflect on places you can write over the summer. • model writing in a journal. • model using writing as a way to remember special summer times. • model how to write letters to keep in touch with students and friends.	• draw and write a writing goal for the summer in their journals. • draw and label pictures of places they can see themselves writing over the summer in their journals. • decorate the cover of their summer writing journals. • make a list of ways they will try writing over the summer in their journals. • write the first page of their journals.
COMMITMENT 1 day	• celebrate and share a way you will write over the summer.	• celebrate their summer writing journals with a partner.
TOTAL: 8 DAYS		

Circular Seasons:
Endings and Beginnings

You will miss these children. And they will miss you. For the rest of their lives, they will remember your name. There should be more of a ritual for you to let go of these children and prepare to embrace the new ones.

In Japan, every fall there is a traditional chrysanthemum festival to celebrate the last blooming before the winter comes. The people journey to view the beautiful flowers and to celebrate the changing seasons. There are special horticulturists who work for a full eleven months of the year to prepare for this festival, creating spectacular chrysanthemum arrangements, which they feature in *uwaya*, serene shelters for the beautiful plantings. In this way, people can contemplate and reflect upon the changing seasons. I wish we had such a thing for the work we do. The seasons go by and then come around again. There is a beauty in that; we know they will always come again. But these, these precious children, they will never come again quite like this. Let these last days of the school year be an *uwaya* for us: a serene shelter for reflection. The work you do with your students is, well, once in a lifetime. Remember this as the seasons of your teaching life begin once again.

Chapter 6

TRACKING STUDENT PROGRESS ACROSS THE YEAR

The C4 Assessment

Assessment is the beginning, the middle, and the end of our teaching. It is the heart of our instruction, the age-old dilemma, the most gratifying, frustrating, and rewarding aspect of our work, because it reveals in stark relief: How are we all doing? Done well, it is not offensive, harmful, hurtful, or unpleasant for children. Done well, it is engaging, reflective, fascinating, and insightful for teachers. Done poorly, it is demeaning, demoralizing, and useless to everyone. Done poorly, it is unhelpful, uninteresting, and slightly boring. We have created rubrics as formative assessments and a yearlong assessment tool we call the C4 Assessment that we believe will lead you to the "done well" column. Done well, assessment is meaningful, as J. Richard Gentry points out (2008), "...you can loop together assessment and instruction and use both simultaneously to support your students in targeted and powerful ways."

Unit Rubrics as Formative Assessments

Within each unit we have written for this book, we have given you a model assessment rubric such as the following:

Unit Assessment Connecting to Story Elements: Reading Fiction			STRATEGY
Student name:	EMERGING	DEVELOPING	INDEPENDENT
Categorizes fiction from nonfiction.			
Describes relationships between characters.			
Identifies differences in uses of time in simple text.			
Describes a problem and solution in story.			

These rubrics can and should be used as formative assessments. By this we mean that you can construct rubrics such as these with your students during the Identification stage of any unit. As you name the expectations for process behaviors, or the elements of a genre, or the type of strategy or convention you would like to see your students use, you can add this list of performance indicators to your rubric. Then you can give the rubric to your students to use during their Guided Practice. If we give students our upfront expectations in writing, and they have helped to form and understand these expectations, we can be sure that they will know what we want them to do as readers and writers. They can use these rubrics as placeholders for our teaching—reminding them on a daily basis what we want them to practice, even when we are not sitting next to them.

By keeping the rubric alongside your conferring conversations with individual readers and writers, you will be able to focus your observations and record your comments on how each student is performing throughout the length of the unit. Using the rubric to supplement your conferring plans will also allow you to refer back on these conversations to plan for future instruction—either for the entire class when you see something that nearly everyone is having difficulty with, or for individual or small-group work.

Unit Rubrics as Summative Assessments

Of course these rubrics can also be summative. You may use them to measure your students' performance at the end of each unit, and you may gather these collective unit assessments to plan and draft your report cards. We believe these rubrics will be extremely helpful on several levels. They will help you focus your instruction toward the expectations listed on the rubric. They will help guide and focus your students practice within any unit of study, and they will allow for self-reflection— for our students and for ourselves. By the end of any unit, we should be able to see what students accomplished and what we still need to work on.

The C4 Assessment

Rubrics are not the only form of assessment that we would like you to consider. As our entire year has been built around the premise of balanced instruction across process, genre, strategy, and conventions, we would like to suggest that you consider your students' growing skills and abilities within these four categories. To help you accomplish this task, we have created the C4 Assessment (C4A) forms seen at the end of this chapter. These forms merge many of the teaching points across the year into collective assessments of students' understanding of process, genre, strategy, and conventions. The C4A is clear and simple to use, and yet provides a great deal of information for teachers, so that we may differentiate our instruction for all students; for parents so we may share students' growth or challenges; and for schools.

Tracking Our Students Across the Grades

We have designed specific C4 assessments for each grade level. While their format and organization are the same, the content varies, as we have given a great deal of thought to the articulation of instruction across the grades. We recommend that these assessment forms be filled out each year and passed on to the next year's teacher. This will give teachers a clearer sense of their students as readers and writers at the beginning of the year than traditional packaged reading or writing assessments.

Using These Forms

There are many different ways to incorporate these forms into your year. You may choose to

- use them to conduct a more formal review of student performance at the beginning, middle, and end of the year.
- keep these forms with your other conferring materials and use them to note when students demonstrate progress within a particular unit.
- keep these forms with you as you read through your students' published writing, so you can use their written work as evidence of learning.

No matter which method you use, we ask you to consider how your children are developing as readers and writers inside the Complete 4 components. What have they learned to do as readers and writers? What have they come to understand about genre? What have they learned about reading and writing strategies? What do they now understand about the world of conventions? Our job is to create lifelong readers and writers in our classrooms. Instruction-linked assessment through the Complete 4 is the key to achieving this objective.

Complete 4 Component: Process Kindergarten

KEY: **E**=emerging **D**=developing **I**=independent

Student: _____   School Year: _____

CAPACITIES:	BEGINNING OF THE YEAR	MIDDLE OF THE YEAR	END OF THE YEAR
Reads familiar text smoothly (fluency).			
Reads independently for 10–15 minutes (stamina).			
Sustains book talk independently for five minutes (stamina).			
Makes wise book choices according to purpose and interest (independence).			
Writes/draws independently for 10–20 minutes (stamina).			
Sustains a selected writing piece over two to three days (stamina).			
Rereads own writing to add on to a picture, revise words, or fix spelling (independence).			
Attempts to spell new words with confidence (independence).			

ROLES:	BEGINNING OF THE YEAR	MIDDLE OF THE YEAR	END OF THE YEAR
Understands role while meeting in conference with a teacher.			
Transitions from whole class to Independent Practice without assistance.			
Selects from two paper choices.			

IDENTITIES:	BEGINNING OF THE YEAR	MIDDLE OF THE YEAR	END OF THE YEAR
Identifies various purposes for reading.			
Expresses ways that he or she has grown as a reader or writer.			
Uses writing to communicate with others (letters, signs).			
Integrates reading and writing capacities into play experiences.			

Complete 4 Component: Process Kindergarten (continued)   KEY: **E**=emerging **D**=developing **I**=independent

Student: School Year:

COLLABORATION:	BEGINNING OF THE YEAR	MIDDLE OF THE YEAR	END OF THE YEAR
Sits knee-to-knee with a partner.			
Makes eye contact with a partner.			
Responds during conversation by nodding and adding ideas.			
Asks questions that relate to the conversation.			
Shares writing ideas, written products, and books with a partner.			
Interacts in positive, supportive ways with a partner.			

Complete 4 Component: Genre Kindergarten

KEY: **E**=emerging **D**=developing **I**=independent

Student: _____   School Year: _____

NARRATIVE:	BEGINNING OF THE YEAR	MIDDLE OF THE YEAR	END OF THE YEAR
Uses information from pictures to tell a familiar story.			
Identifies story elements.			
Describes relationships between characters.			
Identifies problem and solution in a story.			
Distinguishes fiction from nonfiction texts.			
Writes stories with a beginning, middle, and end.			
Writes/tells stories using story elements to develop and sequence the idea.			
Writes/tells imaginative stories with story language.			

NONFICTION:	BEGINNING OF THE YEAR	MIDDLE OF THE YEAR	END OF THE YEAR
Distinguishes fiction from nonfiction texts.			
Writes a label book on one topic of interest.			
Identifies features of nonfiction text (photographs or realistic illustrations, bold words, labels, simple diagrams).			
Understands the purpose of various text features and can access information from them.			
Uses nonfiction text features in his or her own writing.			
Includes an introduction to his or her nonfiction book.			
Writes a nonfiction book on a topic of interest.			

POETRY:	BEGINNING OF THE YEAR	MIDDLE OF THE YEAR	END OF THE YEAR
Distinguishes a poem from a story.			
Recognizes the look of a poem.			
Recognizes the sound of a poem by identifying rhyme or rhythm.			
Recognizes repetition.			
Attempts repetition in his or her own writing (one or two words or lines).			
Describes a simple visual image in one or two lines.			

Complete 4 Component: Strategy Kindergarten

KEY: **E**=emerging **D**=developing **I**=independent

Student: _____ School Year: _____

INPUT (the strategies readers use to comprehend text):	BEGINNING OF THE YEAR	MIDDLE OF THE YEAR	END OF THE YEAR
Takes picture walks to access story information.			
Identifies story elements.			
Recalls one scene from a story and retells it accurately.			
Retells a familiar story through its story elements.			
Retells sequentially.			
Makes simple predictions based on visual cues and knowledge of character.			
Connects at least two texts based on similarities or differences in problem/solution, setting, or character.			
Uses rereading as a strategy to figure out an unknown word or to clarify confusion in comprehension.			
Uses various strategies to read a new word.			

OUTPUT (the strategies writers use to create text):	BEGINNING OF THE YEAR	MIDDLE OF THE YEAR	END OF THE YEAR
Writes about a character, real or imagined.			
Describes a simple setting.			
Tells a story with all story elements (through play, pictures, words—written or oral).			
Creates a story plan using picture cues.			
Uses multiple pages to plan a story or topic idea.			
Generates writing ideas.			
Uses a set of spelling strategies to write unknown words.			
Adds onto a story with color, details in a picture, label, or one to two sentences.			
Adds titles to written work.			
Adds page numbers to written work.			

Complete 4 Component: Conventions Kindergarten   KEY: **E**=emerging **D**=developing **I**=independent

Student: School Year:

SYNTAX:	BEGINNING OF THE YEAR	MIDDLE OF THE YEAR	END OF THE YEAR
Writes sentences with subject/verb agreement with support.			
Shows evidence of adjective awareness.			

PUNCTUATION:	BEGINNING OF THE YEAR	MIDDLE OF THE YEAR	END OF THE YEAR
Recognizes question marks in text by altering vocal quality.			
Uses exclamation points and question marks.			
Capitalizes letters at the beginning of sentences 80 percent of the time.			
Uses periods at the end of sentences 80 percent of the time.			

SPELLING/DECODING:	BEGINNING OF THE YEAR	MIDDLE OF THE YEAR	END OF THE YEAR
Recognizes and writes beginning consonants.			
Recognizes and writes middle consonants.			
Recognizes and writes ending consonants.			
Writes all vowel sounds (except blends and "y").			
Recognizes and writes all letters of the alphabet in lowercase.			
Recognizes and writes all letters of the alphabet in uppercase.			
Incorporates known sight words into writing.			
Writes own name.			
Recognizes and writes at least three names of classroom community members.			

Chapter 7

Essential Reading for the Complete 4 Educator

The Complete 4 for Literacy
by Pam Allyn

Pam's book *The Complete 4 for Literacy* introduces us to the idea of the four major components for literacy instruction: Process, Genre, Strategy, and Conventions. She illuminates the components and how they interact throughout the year. In your school communities, we encourage you to form study groups around these components. Begin with Pam's book and study it together to orient yourself. Then, each year or each season, select one of the components to focus on. We can use each component to discuss not just whole-class instruction but also how best to confer with individual students, how to work with struggling readers and writers, and how to assess our students. We have prepared a special selection of professional texts to foster your investigation of each of the components.

Writing Above Standard
by Debbie Lera

Debbie Lera will help you to frame a year of teaching writing that really helps your students soar using your state standards as a guide. With the Complete 4 as the backbone of her thinking, Debbie takes us on a journey through state standards and how to make them work for us. In the spirit of the Complete 4 and the Complete Year which is all about building flexible frameworks, this book furthers your thinking by helping you to benefit from the structure provided by the standards while attending to the individual needs of your students.

Professional Books on Process

There are wonderful books in the field of the teaching of reading and writing that help remind us why process work is so critical. Learning routines, talking about books, choosing topics: these activities form the bedrock of a lifetime of success as readers and writers. Remind yourself that process is the key to a happy life—how you live your life is as important as what you do with it. Some of our favorites include:

- *The Boy Who Would Be a Helicopter* by Vivien Paley

- *A Fresh Look at Writing* by Donald Graves

- *Kindergarten Literacy* by Cindy Middendorf

- *The Literate Kindergarten: Where Wonder and Discovery Thrive* by Susan L. Kempton

- *Reading and Writing in Kindergarten: A Practical Guide* by Rosalie Franzese

- *Wally's Stories* by Vivien Paley

Bonus: *Children's Books and Their Creators* edited by Anita Silvey. A must-have for your shelf! It is a detailed collection of great authors' biographies and also excerpts from their most famous books. There is a lot of author information here that is excellent to incorporate into "where writers get ideas" lessons.

Professional Books on Genre

Kindergarteners are capable of doing so much and are very proud of themselves for being like the big kids. Genre units allow our kindergarteners to try on many hats and be in the world of reading and writing. Genre is a powerful tool. If you know which genre matches your purpose, you can communicate more effectively. Helpful books for your learning include:

- *For the Good of the Earth and Sun* by Georgia Heard (poetry)

- *Is That a Fact?* by Tony Stead (nonfiction)

- *Keepsakes: Using Family Stories in Elementary Classrooms* by Linda Winston (narrative)

Professional Books on Strategy

In this book, you can see how strongly we believe in the strategic mind of the kindergartener! In his play, the kindergartener is thoughtful and bases his decisions on the whole of his idea. So, too, we can help our students become strategic as readers and writers. The following books contain some helpful information on strategy work:

- *Craft Lessons* by Ralph Fletcher

- *Differentiating Instruction in Kindergarten* by Cindy Middendorf

- *Don't Speed. Read! 12 Steps to Smart and Sensible Fluency Instruction* by Michael F. Opitz

- *Fluency in Focus: Comprehension Strategies for All Young Readers* by Mary Lee Prescott-Griffin and Nancy I. Witherell

- *Read It Again* by Brenda Parkes

- *Reading With Meaning* by Debbie Miller

- *Teaching for Comprehension in Reading, Grades K–2* by Gay Su Pinnell and Patricia L. Scharer

Professional Books on Conventions

We are lucky that in these last few years, there's been an explosion of interesting perspectives on conventions: grammar, punctuation, and syntax. This is the hardest hurdle for us to overcome; most of us grew up remembering either no grammar instruction or terrible grammar instruction. Spelling and grammar and punctuation can all be fun, truly! Conventions instruction is empowering and students want to learn how to spell. They want to be in on the secrets of language.

- *Mastering the Mechanics: Modeled, Guided, and Independent Editing, K–1* by Linda Hoyt and Teresa Therriault

- *Spelling K–8* by Gay Su Pinnell and Irene Fountas

- *Spelling in Use* by Lester Laminack and Katie Wood Ray

- *You Kan Red This* by Sandra Wilde

Resource Sheets

Early Fall

- Resource 2.1   Alphabet Chart
- Resource 2.2   Personalizing Writing Folders
- Resource 2.3   Parent Letter: An Introduction to Reading and Telling
                      Stories Through Pictures
- Resource 2.4   Directions for Making Your Own Story Strings
- Resource 2.5   Directions for Making Your Own Story Cubes
- Resource 2.6   Storytelling Homework
- Resource 2.7   Share a Special Object Homework
- Resources 2.8–2.11 Paper Samples for Early Fall Units

Late Fall/Early Winter

- Resource 3.1   Parent Letter: An Introduction to
                      the Conventions Units
- Resource 3.2   Labeling Homework
- Resources 3.3–3.6   Paper Samples for Late Fall/Early Winter Units

Winter

- Resource 4.1   Parent Letter: An Introduction to the Strategy Units
- Resource 4.2   Speech Bubble Template
- Resource 4.3   Learning by Imitating Homework
- Resources 4.4–4.7   Paper Samples for Winter Units

Spring

- Resource 5.1   Parent Letter: An Introduction to Nonfiction Reading
                      and Writing
- Resources 5.2–5.5   Paper Samples for Spring Units

Alphabet Chart

Ee	Dd	Cc	Bb	Aa
Jj	Ii	Hh	Gg	Ff
Oo	Nn	Mm	Ll	Kl
Tt	Ss	Rr	Qq	Pp
Yy	Xx	Ww	Vv	Uu
tr	th	sh	ch	Zz

Personalizing Writing Folders

Students decorate the outside of their writing folders with photos, words, and illustrations that have special meaning. Photos of family members, pets, and friends may be glued on the folders.

The inside pockets are marked with a red dot on one side and a green one on the other. Completed writing pieces go in the red-dot pocket while ongoing writing goes in the green-dot pocket.

An Introduction to Reading and Telling Stories Through Pictures

Dear Parents,

We have recently begun a new study in reading and writing focusing on story elements, which we will call "story ingredients." These include character, setting, and plot (or important things that happen in the story).

An important precursor to writing a story is knowing how to *tell* a good story.

Here are ways to support your child's learning at home:

- Tell the story of a familiar picture book together by looking at the pictures.

- Name the story ingredients in a book.

- Look for familiar letters or words on a page.

- Say the letters in a word.

- Tell stories to your child based on memories that you have, or make up a story.

- Include other family members. Call a grandparent or other relative and ask him or her to tell your child a story.

- Start a story (real or imagined) and ask your child to continue it.

Our "Treasure Tell" will begin next week. Children are encouraged to bring in an object from home and share it with the class by telling a story that goes with the object. Urge your children to bring treasures that have stories inside them: a special stuffed animal, a shell, or a postcard. Your child should practice telling the story the day before he or she is to share in class. I will send home a Treasure Tell schedule so you know when your child will be sharing.

I am looking for guest storytellers to visit the classroom. If you or another family member is interested, please let me know. We would love to have you!

Sincerely,

Directions for Making Your Own Story Strings

Materials List

yarn, hot glue gun, buttons or laminated pictures to represent different story elements

Choosing the Character and Setting Buttons or Pictures

- Character icon
  - You can either use the same icon for all strings or use different ones, showing students a variety of characters as they use different strings. Some possibilities for this icon include a child, an animal, an adult, or a grandparent.

- Setting icon
  - You can either use the same icon for all the strings or use different ones, showing students a variety of settings as they use different strings. Some possibilities for this icon include a castle, barn, house, or school.

Making the String

- Start with thick yarn or string. Braid into a thick rope of approximately 12 inches.

- Gather buttons or small laminated pictures to represent story elements. Hot-glue the icons in the following order:
  - character icon
  - setting icon
  - two blank buttons or circles to represent important events in the story
  - a bow to represent the "tie-up," or ending of a story

Variations of the String

Story Strings with buttons look beautiful and are durable. However, they can be costly. Creative teachers we work with have come up with cost-effective alternatives to our Story String.

Story Stick

Gather paint sticks or craft sticks. Glue laminated pictures onto the stick.

My Story String

Purchase blank Shrinky Dink paper. Students draw their own story element icons; they are then baked and glued onto braided strings.

Directions for Making Your Own Story Cubes

Materials List

two cube-shaped boxes, wrapping paper, character pictures, setting pictures, glue, clear adhesive paper

Character Pictures

Collect pictures for the character cube. The character pictures you choose should represent both fictional and real people. Possibilities include baby, grandmother, child, teacher, firefighter, alien, princess, unicorn, pirate, dinosaur. Paste one picture on each face of the cube.

Setting Pictures

Collect pictures for the setting cube. The setting pictures you choose should represent both fictional and real settings. Possibilities include a city scene, a barnyard, a school, the moon, a castle, a forest, playground, a bedroom, a jungle, a desert. Paste one picture on each face of the cube.

Making the Story Cubes

- Gather two cube-shaped boxes. One box will be a character cube, the other a setting cube.
- Wrap boxes with paper.
- Glue one character picture on each face of the character cube.
- Glue one setting picture on each face of the setting cube.
- Wrap each cube in clear adhesive paper.

Storytelling Homework

For homework this week, tell one story a day to someone at home. Your story might be about something that happened at school, or it might be a story from your imagination. Record who you told your story to and make a sketch of one part of your story.

Monday I told a story to _____.	**Tuesday** I told a story to _____.
Wednesday I told a story to _____.	**Thursday** I told a story to _____.

Name _____ Date _____

Share a Special Object Homework Assignment

We read *Wilfrid Gordon McDonald Partridge* by Mem Fox today. It is about a boy who helps a friend remember stories from her life by showing her different objects.

We are learning how to tell stories in school. Please find one object (or photograph) at home that has a story you can tell about it—like Miss Nancy did in our book. Practice telling the story to someone at home tonight and remember to mix in our story ingredients to make the story interesting and clear.

Please bring your object to school tomorrow. You will tell your story to your partner at writing time.

Story Ingredients:

Characters—tell who is in your story

Setting—tell where the story is taking place

Events—tell about three important things that happen

Name _____

Date _____

RESOURCE 2.8

Name _____ Date _____

Name

Date

RESOURCE 2.10

Name _____ Date _____

An Introduction to the Conventions Units

Dear Parents,

This is a very exciting time in your child's development, as he or she is just becoming aware of the world of written language. We are embarking on a unit that focuses on print in picture books. Your child will be reading and writing these kinds of books, too. We will explore how writers use effective spelling strategies to tackle the writing of print in their books. We want this work to feel joyful and safe. We will be studying both sound- and sight-based spelling strategies. To spell by sound, writers stretch the sounds in a word and write what they hear. Sight strategies include closing one's eyes and visualizing the word one wants to write, as well as copying print that is displayed in the environment.

Your children are becoming more aware of print on the page. We have talked about readers being like detectives—discovering clues that will enable them to read the words on the page. At home, as you are reading together, stop and model your own process as a reading detective when you encounter challenging words.

I look forward to a rich two weeks of learning in this unit.

Sincerely,

Name _____ Date _____

Labeling Homework

We are reading books in class that have labels. This week for homework, make a drawing of something in your home—your bedroom, a pet, a special toy. Add at least two labels to your drawing. If you do not want to make a drawing, you can glue a photograph onto paper and label that.

Name _____

Date _____

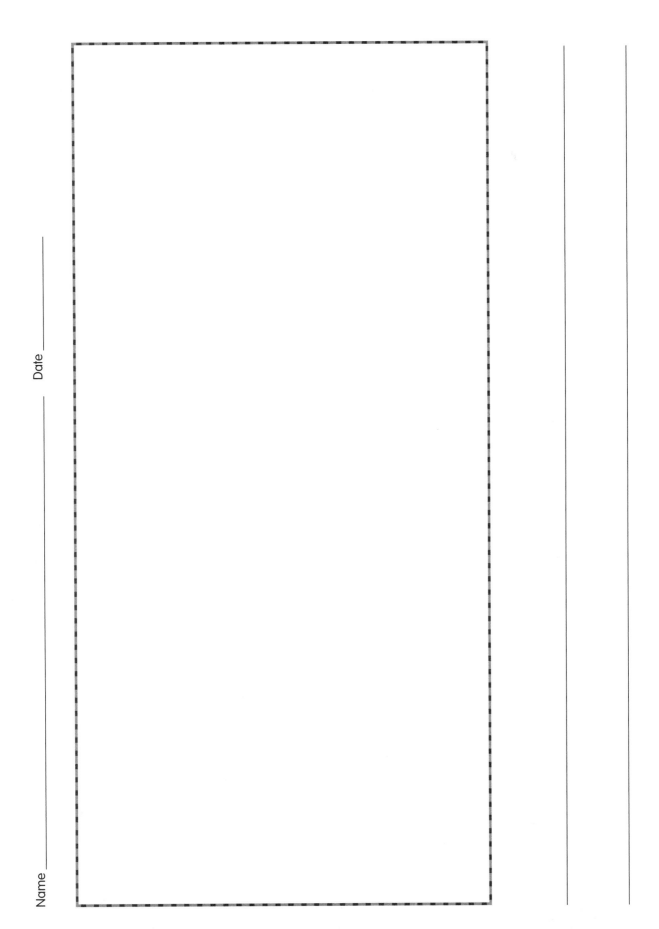

RESOURCE 3.3

Name _____ Date _____

Name _____ Date _____

An Introduction to the Strategy Units

Dear Parents,

The children are retelling stories they have heard me read in class. The familiarity of these stories enables the children to focus on identifying and including specific "ingredients" in their retellings.

To support this learning at home, revisit a familiar, favorite story with your child. Talk about what happened in the story. Take turns retelling it. It may also be fun for your child to retell a book over the telephone to a family member or friend who may not live close by.

Thank you for the ongoing support and encouragement you give to your child on a daily basis. Feel free to contact me with any questions or concerns.

Warmly,

Name _____ Date _____

Speech Bubble Template

Name _____   Date _____

Learning by Imitating: Homework Assignment

At writing time, we discussed how imitation is a great way to learn something new. We have all learned by imitating others. Today we talked, drew pictures, and wrote about our own experiences of learning through imitating.

Ask a grown-up or sibling at home about what s/he has learned by imitating someone. Talk about what was learned and who he or she learned from.

I talked to _____

She learned how to _____

_____

_____

by imitating _____

_____.

Name _____ Date _____

Name _____ Date _____

_____

_____

Name _____ Date _____

_____

_____

_____

_____

Name _____ Date _____

_____

_____

_____

_____

_____

_____

_____

_____

_____

RESOURCE 4.7

An Introduction to Nonfiction Reading and Writing

Dear Parents,

For the next few weeks, your children will study how nonfiction texts are different from fiction. When you go to the library (or even at home), ask your child to help you sort nonfiction books from fiction books.

They will also learn how to gain information from books when they cannot read the main body of text—through text features such as photographs and labeled pictures. Your child will incorporate what she is learning about reading nonfiction books into a nonfiction book that she will write.

It will be helpful if you can talk to your child about the nonfiction reading and writing you do in your own life. This may include reading a newspaper, a book on a topic you are interested in, cookbooks, manuals, or the grocery store circular. Reflect on informational writing you may have done: work-related writing, instructions for a babysitter, or directions to get somewhere.

Your child is curious and excited about the world. Together, we can encourage your child to be curious and full of wonder and open to questions and seeking answers. This is what nonfiction is all about!

Warmly,

Name _____ Date _____

My Passions

_____

_____

_____

Name

Date

RESOURCE 5.3

Name _____ Date _____

Name _____ Date _____

```
┌ ─ ─ ─ ─ ─ ─ ─ ─ ─ ─ ─ ─ ─ ─ ─ ─ ─ ─ ┐
|                                      |
|                                      |
|                                      |
|                                      |
|                                      |
|                                      |
|                                      |
|                                      |
|                                      |
|                                      |
└ ─ ─ ─ ─ ─ ─ ─ ─ ─ ─ ─ ─ ─ ─ ─ ─ ─ ─ ┘
```

_____

_____

_____

_____

_____

Glossary of Terms for the Complete Year Series

We try to avoid jargon as much as possible, but it is inevitable that a community creates or uses specific terminology to identify important aspects of its work. We want you to feel comfortable with all the language inside this book. What follows are some of the key words we have used throughout this book and throughout the Complete Year series.

Anchor texts These are the books that moor us to the places of our learning. An anchor holds a ship in place, in water that may be moving fast. Texts are like that for us in our teaching. We are in moving water all the time, but great literature anchors us down to our teaching, to our learning, to our goals and outcomes. Anchor texts connect us to the teaching inside our units of study. They keep our teaching on course, steady, focused, anchoring our big ideas, our commitments and indeed, the essence of each unit. Anchor texts may also be used throughout the year in both the teaching of reading and the teaching of writing. For example, one text may be used in a reading unit for retelling, or sensory image, or prediction. The same text may also be used as a demonstration text for writing with detail, strong leads and endings, and the use of dialogue. There are some special texts that can travel with you throughout the year. They are great, lasting titles that transcend any one teaching point. These are considered anchor texts for the year.

Book clubs Working in book clubs allows students to build their collaboration skills and their ability to talk about texts. Book clubs may form from two sets of successful partnerships, or for a variety of teaching purposes. You may group a club according to skill sets or according to interests. Students in a club do not all have to be reading the same book. For example, in a nonfiction unit, the students may meet to discuss editorials or historical writing, using different texts at their own reading levels. You should give clear guidelines for the purposes of a club, its duration, expected outcomes, and how it will be assessed.

Commitment The fourth stage of a unit of study, the Commitment stage, is the bridge from the end of one unit to the beginning of the next one. Look for and make public examples of student work and behaviors that are becoming more integrated into the ongoing work of the individual and the community.

This stage asks the question: How is what we have learned in this unit going to inform our learning as we begin the next one? It also requires a response to the question: What have you learned?

Conferences/conferring This is a process for informally assessing your students' progress, and for differentiating your instruction for individual readers and writers. Ideally, you will meet with each student at least once a week in a brief, focused conference session. Stages of a conference are:

- **Preread/Research** (be very familiar with your student's work and processes in advance of the conference)
- **Ask** (pertinent questions relating to your lesson, the ongoing work, and the plans going forward)
- **Listen** (take notes, with attention to next steps)
- **Teach** (one target point)
- **Plan** (what the student will do when you leave the conference: today, tomorrow, throughout the unit and the year)

Conventions The fourth component of the Complete 4, Conventions refers to grammar, punctuation, and syntax. Understanding the conventions of the English language has a direct impact on reading comprehension and writing mechanics and fluency.

Downhill texts These are texts we can rest and relax into—to practice building our stamina or our fluency or to revisit favorite characters, authors, or series. They are books that do not require a great deal of decoding to be done by the reader, as the text is generally below the reader's independent reading level.

Focused Instruction The first part of every day's reading and writing time, Focused Instruction is the short, focused lesson at the beginning of each workshop session in the teaching of reading or writing. Each lesson should build on the ones before it. No lesson is taught in isolation.

Four Prompts In order to help our students learn how to find ideas for writing, we have developed a set of prompts to guide them. They are I wonder, I remember, I observe, and I imagine. You can use these to support your students' writing in any genre.

Genre The second component of the Complete 4, Genre typically refers to a type of text such as poetry, nonfiction, or narrative. Within each of these genres are subgenres, which may include a specific focus on persuasive nonfiction writing, or informational nonfiction writing in nonfiction studies. In a narrative study, the focus might be on the short story, the memoir, or story elements. We want students to focus on how they engage with a particular genre. How do we read a newspaper, for example, and how do we read a poem? How are they different, and how are they the same? We will talk about uses for a genre, the reasons we read inside one genre for a length of time, and how our thinking grows and changes as a result of that immersion.

Guided Practice In the third stage of any unit of study, Guided Practice, we use mentor texts, transcripts, teacher or student writing, think-alouds, role plays, and read-alouds to model exemplary attributes, behaviors, and qualities related to the unit. Over the course of this stage, students are given increasing responsibility for this work. It is generally the longest stage of a unit, as all students need time for practice.

Identification The second stage of any unit of study, Identification, is the time when we begin to develop the common language we will use throughout the study. We identify attributes of a genre, behaviors in a process, qualities of a craft element, rules for a convention or mark. Our thinking is recorded in public charts, student writing notebooks, and our notebook.

Immersion The first stage of any unit of study, Immersion, is the initial period of inquiry during which we surround our students with the sounds, textures, and qualities of a Genre, Process, Strategy, or Conventions focus. We marinate our students in the literature, the actions and reflections, and the attention to detail and conventions that are part of the study. During this stage, students construct a working understanding of the topic under discussion.

Independent Practice Following each day's Focused Instruction, Independent Practice provides time for students to read or write independently and authentically. Students independently read a variety of texts matched to their reading levels. Students also write a variety of texts independently, depending on the unit and their ability levels. They practice the skills and strategies taught in the whole-group sessions. We provide daily lessons to support their work, and confer regularly with the students to assess their individual needs.

Mentor text Somewhat interchangeable with an anchor text, we are more inclined to use mentor text to describe books that have particular appeal to individual students. Mentor texts inspire students' reading and writing, whereas anchor texts are specific texts chosen in advance by the teacher to prepare a unit. So in a poetry unit, one mentor text might be a Langston Hughes poem, "The Dream Keeper," because the student loves it and wants to write like that, whereas another student might choose a Valerie Worth poem because she likes the brevity of her language.

Partnerships At times you may choose to pair children for different reasons and different lengths of time. Partnerships can be very fluid, lasting for just one session, a week, or an entire unit. Partnerships may be based on reading levels, similar interests in particular books or subjects, or because you would like to work with the partners on a regular basis on small instructional reading or writing work.

Process The first of the Complete 4 components, Process asks readers and writers to become aware of their habits and behaviors, and to move forward in developing them. Process units can investigate roles, routines, capacity, or collaboration.

Read-aloud During read-aloud, you read from carefully chosen texts that reflect the reading and writing work the community is doing together. Listening to fluent and expressive read-alouds helps students identify the many aspects of text and develop their own deeper understandings of Process, Genre, Strategy, or Conventions. You may read from a book or short text that illustrates the topic of the Focused Instruction for the day, and encourage students to pursue that thinking in their independent reading and writing. During and at the end of the read-aloud, the whole class may have a conversation relating to the ideas in the story.

Reading notebook *See* Writing Notebook.

Shared reading/shared writing During this activity, you and your students read together from a shared text (on an overhead, chart, or a SMART Board, or using copies of the text). While teachers of younger children use shared reading and writing to help build decoding skills, teachers of older children may use shared reading to teach word analysis, new vocabulary, or punctuation skills. It's also a good way to work with older students on big-picture thinking such as developing an idea about a text, asking questions, or making inferences. Teachers of older students may use shared writing to guide their students toward new writing strategies in a public writing context, or model use of details and elaboration to improve their writing.

Small instructional groups This structure is used to differentiate and direct instruction to the specific needs of a small group of learners. You pull small groups of readers or writers with similar needs to explicitly teach targeted reading and writing skills. You select and introduce the texts for reading and make specific teaching points. You may prompt students in small writing groups to do a short, focused writing exercise based on their needs. These groups are flexible and will change as the year unfolds.

Stages of the lesson Each day, we should work with our students in a whole-small-whole routine. First we bring everyone together for the lesson (see Focused Instruction), then we send students off to practice something we have taught (see Independent Practice), and finally we call them back to join us for a recap and reiteration of our teaching (see Wrap-Up).

Stages of the unit Each unit of study follows a progression of instruction, from Immersion to Identification to Guided Practice to Commitment. These stages provide students with the necessary opportunities to notice, name, practice, and share their learning—all of which contribute to a deeper understanding and application of our teaching (see Immersion, Identification, Guided Practice, and Commitment).

Steady reader or writer This student is making steady progress and meeting appropriate grade-level expectations.

Strategy The third component in the Complete 4, Strategy consists of two types: reading and writing. In reading, Strategy refers to individual or grouped strategies for reading comprehension that impact reading development. These include visualizing, synthesizing, questioning, and inferring. A unit focused on strategy can be embedded in another study or illuminated on its own. Strategy units also include the study of theme, interpretation, building an argument, and story elements. In writing, Strategy refers to craft. This may include the external or internal structures of writing. Units in writing strategy may include structures of nonfiction or narrative texts, a focus on a particular author, or, internally, units focused on the use of repetition, varied sentence length, or the artful use of punctuation.

Strong reader or writer This student is performing above grade-level expectations.

Turn and talk This common technique helps students warm up for their reading or writing

work. By asking students to "turn and talk" to someone in the meeting area to rehearse their thoughts, we give all students a chance to have their voices heard. It is an effective management technique for making sure students are prepared for the work ahead.

Unit of study A one- to six-week period of intensive study on one aspect of reading or writing. The Complete 4 curriculum planning system helps teachers and administrators plan an entire school year in the teaching of reading and writing.

Uphill texts This descriptor refers to a text that is above a student's independent reading level. Sometimes we want our readers to challenge themselves with a harder text. Sometimes readers have very good reasons for why they would like to keep an uphill book close by. Other times, though, we ask them to recognize that the book is too uphill for the task, and that they need to find a level text with which they can feel successful.

Vulnerable reader or writer This describes the reader or writer who struggles to keep up with the demands of the grade level. These are students who need extra support and scaffolding through appropriate texts or individualized or small-group instruction. Our vulnerable readers and writers need special care to feel successful and to flourish in our classrooms.

Wrap-Up The final step in each day's reading or writing time, the Wrap-Up is when we ask our students to return to a whole-group setting for reflection and reinforcement. For example, you may share one or two examples of student work or student behaviors ("Today I noticed..."), or one or two students might briefly share their thinking processes or the work itself.

Writing clubs These are recommended for all ages. Children may create clubs based on common interests, from the block area and writing in kindergarten to mystery writing in fourth grade. Give clear guidelines for the purposes of the clubs, the length of time they will last, the expectations, the outcomes, and how you will assess the progress of each club.

Writing notebook/reading notebook/ writing folder/reading folder These are containers for thinking and tools for collecting ideas, wonderings, observations, questions, research, lists, snippets of texts, and responses to literature. The form of the container is not the important thing; what is important is having containers for student work that make sense to your students and work well for you in terms of collecting and preserving a history of student reading and writing.

Kindergarten Anchor Texts

Early Fall

The ARCH: Home/School Connections in Reading

- *A Bedtime Story* by Mem Fox
- *A Box Full of Kittens* by Sonia Manzano
- *My Kindergarten* by Rosemary Wells
- *The Napping House* by Audrey Wood
- *Please, Puppy, Please* by Spike Lee and Tanya Lewis Lee
- *Reading Makes You Feel Good* by Todd Parr
- *Rescue Vehicles* by Robert Gould

The ARCH: Home/School Connections in Writing

- *A Box Full of Kittens* by Sonia Manzano
- *Goodnight, Moon* by Margaret Wise Brown
- *I Want to Be* by Thylias Moss
- *Koala Lou* by Mem Fox
- *My Kindergarten* by Rosemary Wells
- *The Napping House* by Audrey Wood

Reading Stories Through Pictures

- *The Gingerbread Man* by Catherine McCafferty
- *Goldilocks and the Three Bears* by Byron Barton
- *How Rabbit Tricked Otter* by Gayle Ross
- *Jack and the Beanstalk* by Carol Ottelenghi
- *Kiss Good Night* by Amy Hest
- *The Kissing Hand* by Audrey Penn
- *Mama Panya's Pancakes: A Village Tale From Kenya* by Mary Chamberlin
- *The Three Billy Goats Gruff* by Stephen Carpenter

- *The Three Little Pigs* by Patricia Siebert
- *Where the Wild Things Are* by Maurice Sendak
- *Yeh-Shen: A Cinderella Story from China* by Ai-Ling Louie

Telling Stories Through Pictures and Words

- *Bedtime for Frances* by Russell Hoban
- *Calabash Cat* by James Rumford
- *Pablo's Tree* by Pat Mora
- *The Paper Bag Princess* by Robert Munsch
- *A Snowy Surprise* by Amy Hest
- *Superhero* by Marc Tauss
- *Tell Me a Story, Mama* by Angela Johnson and David Soman
- *Wilfrid Gordon McDonald Partridge* by Mem Fox
- *William's Doll* by Charlotte Zolotow

Reading for Many Purposes: Connecting Books to Play

- *Castle* by David McCauley
- Walt Disney's *Cinderella*
- *Madlenka* by Peter Sis
- *Whistle for Willie* by Ezra Jack Keats

Writing for Many Purposes: Connecting Writing to Play

- *Fancy Nancy* by Robin Preiss Glasser
- *Frog and Toad Together* by Arnold Lobel
- *I Wanna Iguana* by Karen Kaufman Orloff
- *The Jolly Postman* by Allan Ahlberg
- *Signs in Our World* by DK Publishing
- *What a Wonderful World* by Bob Thiele

Late Fall

Reading Words With Confidence: Using Decoding Strategies

- *The Big Book of Words for Curious Kids* by Heloise Antoine
- *Cassie's Word Quilt* by Faith Ringgold
- *First the Egg* by Laura Vaccaro Seeger
- *Garden Friends* by DK Publishing
- *Growing Vegetable Soup* by Lois Ehlert
- *Jack's Garden* by Henry Cole
- *My First Body Board Book: Spanish/English* by DK Publishing
- *My First Farm Board Book: Spanish/English* by DK Publishing
- *My First Word Book* by DK Publishing
- *Snowballs* by Lois Ehlert
- *Tools* by Taro Miura
- *Vegetables* by Sara Andersen

Writing Words Without Worry: Using Spelling Strategies

- *Cassie's Word Quilt* by Faith Ringgold
- *First Word Book* by Mandy Stanley
- *My Big Truck Book* by Roger Priddy
- *Vegetables* by Sara Anderson

Deepening Capacity for Talk: Reading Partnerships

- *Cross-County* by Mary Calhoun
- *Harold and the Purple Crayon* by Crockett Johnson
- *Where Did You Get Your Moccasins?* by Bernelda Wheeler

Deepening Capacity for Talk: Writing Partnerships

- *Ernest and Celestine's Picnic* by Gabrielle Vincent
- *A Splendid Friend Indeed* by Suzanne Bloom

Exploring the World of Genres: A Reading Unit

- *Amazing Grace* by Mary Hoffman
- *Giant Earth Movers* by Robert Gould
- *Oil Spill!* By Melvin Berger and Paul Mirocha
- *Sing a Song of Popcorn* selected by Beatrice Schenk de Regniers
- *Tacky the Penguin* by Helen Lester

Exploring the World of Genres: A Writing Unit

- *Giant Earth Movers* by Robert Gould
- *Sing a Song of Popcorn* selected by Beatrice Schenk de Regniers
- *Tacky the Penguin* by Helen Lester

Making Choices as Readers

- *Look Out for Turtles* by Melvin Berger
- *My Father's Hands* by Joanne Ryder
- *The Sun Is So Quiet* by Nikki Giovanni
- *Tell Me a Story, Mama* by Angela Johnson

Making Choices as Writers: The Four Prompts

- *Look Out for Turtles* by Melvin Berger
- *My Father's Hands* by Joanne Ryder
- *Some Dogs Do* by Jez Alborough
- *The Sun Is So Quiet* by Nikki Giovanni
- *Tell Me a Story Mama* by Angela Johnson

Winter

Building Stamina: Reading Long and Strong

- *Alice, the Fairy* by David Shannon
- *Bear Snores On* by Karma Wilson
- *A Box Full of Kittens* by Sonia Manzano
- *Shy Charles* by Rosemary Wells
- *A Snowy Surprise* by Amy Hest
- *Strega Nona* by Tomie dePaola

Building Stamina: Writing Long and Strong

- *My Father's Hands* by Joanne Ryder
- *Please, Baby, Please* by Spike Lee and Tanya Lewis Lee

Retelling Using Story Elements

- *Caps for Sale* by Esphyr Slobodkina
- *For You Are a Kenyan Child* by Kelly Cunnane
- *The Road to Mumbai* by Ruth Jeyaveeran
- *Sylvester and the Magic Pebble* by William Steig
- *Tacky the Penguin* by Helen Lester
- *Wemberly Worried* by Kevin Henkes

Revisiting a Favorite Text to Inspire Writing

- *Knuffle Bunny* by Mo Willems
- *The Napping House* by Audrey Wood
- *Peter's Chair* by Ezra Jack Keats
- *Shortcut* by Donald Crews
- *Where the Wild Things Are* by Maurice Sendak

Reading With Fluency: Using Chants, Rhymes, and Other Silly Stuff

- *Arroz Con Leche: Popular Songs and Rhymes from Latin America* by Lulu Delacre

- "Books" by Eloise Greenfield from *In The Land of Words*
- *Little Dog Poems* by Kristine O'Connell George
- "Lollipop" by Ruth Belov Gross
- "Popsicle" by Joan Bransfield Graham from *Splish Splash*
- "School Bus" and "Sliding Board" by Kay Winters from *Did You See What I Saw?*
- "Things" and "Rope Rhyme" by Eloise Greenfield from *Honey I Love and Other Love Poems*

Blooming Poets: A Writing Unit

- *Arroz Con Leche: Popular Songs and Rhymes from Latin America* by Lulu Delacre
- "Behold the Bold Umbrellaphant" from *Behold the Bold Umbrellaphant* by Jack Prelutsky
- "Books," "Nathaniel's Rap," and "New Baby Poem" by Eloise Greenfield from *In The Land of Words*
- *Little Dog Poems* by Kristine O'Connell George
- "Lollipop" by Ruth Belov Gross
- "Popsicle" by Joan Bransfield Graham from *Splish Splash*
- "School Bus" and "Sliding Board" by Kay Winters from *Did You See What I Saw?*
- "Things" and "Rope Rhyme" by Eloise Greenfield from *Honey I Love and Other Love Poems*

Deepening Understanding: Essential Reading Strategies

- *My Kindergarten* by Rosemary Wells
- *Olivia Saves the Circus* by Ian Falconer

- *Senor Cat's Romance ad Other Favorite Stories From Latin America* by Lucia M. Gonzalez
- *Stellaluna* by Janell Cannon

Deepening Meaning: Essential Writing Strategies

- *Black Cat* by Christopher Myers
- *Senor Cat's Romance and Other Favorite Stories from Latin America* by Lucia M. Gonzalez
- *Snowy Surprise* by Amy Hest

Spring

Exploring Many Worlds: Nonfiction Reading

- *Actual Size* by Steve Jenkins
- *Bats* by Gail Gibbons
- *Bears* by Daniel Wood
- *Busy as a Bee* by Melvin Berger (big book)
- *Chameleons Are Cool* by Martin Jenkins
- *Dinosaur ABC* by Roger Priddy
- *Farm Animals* by DK Readers
- *Fire! Fire!* by Gail Gibbons
- *Garden Friends* by DK Readers
- *Growing Vegetable Soup* by Lois Ehlert
- *Jazz on a Saturday Night* by Leo Dillon
- *Little Bear* by Else Homelund Minarik
- *Red Leaf, Yellow Leaf* by Lois Ehlert
- *Spiders* by Gail Gibbons
- *Stellaluna* by Janell Canno
- *Stone Soup* by Jon Murth
- *The Story of Ruby Bridges* by Robert Coles
- *The Very Busy Spider* by Eric Carle
- *Who Lives in the Sea?* by Sylvia M. James (big book)
- *Why Do Leaves Change Color?* by Betsy Maestro

Knowing and Sharing: Nonfiction Writing

- *Apples* by Gilda Berger and Melvin Berger
- *Busy as a Bee* by Melvin Berger
- *Chameleons Are Cool* by Martin Jenkins
- *Chameleon's Colors* by Chisato Tashiro
- *Dogs* by Gail Gibbons
- *Fire! Fire!* by Gail Gibbons
- *Garden Friends* by DK Publishing
- *Harry the Dirty Dog* by Gene Zion
- *I Love Tennis* by DK Publishing
- *Leaves* by Gilda Berger and Melvin Berger
- *Meet the Dinosaurs* by DK Publishing
- *Rules Help* by Marvin Buckley
- *The Ultimate Playground and Recess Game Book* by Guy Bailey

Reading With Expression: Using Punctuation to Enhance Fluency

- *Daniel's Pet* by Alma Flor Ada
- *Green Eggs and Ham* by Dr. Seuss
- *Mrs. Wishy Washy* by Joy Cowley
- *A Splendid Friend Indeed* by Suzanne Bloom
- *There Is a Bird on Your Head* by Mo Willems

Writing With Expression: Using Ending Punctuation to Enhance Meaning

- *Daniel's Pet* by Alma Flor Ada
- *David Goes to School* by David Shannon
- *I Love My New Toy!* by Mo Willems
- *Shortcut* by Donald Crews

Connecting to Story Elements: Reading Fiction

- *Hey, Al!* by Arthur Yorinks

- *Little Gorilla* by Ruth Bornstein
- *Max and Ruby* by Rosemary Wells
- *Olivia Saves the Circus* by Ian Falconer
- *Owen* by Kevin Henkes
- *The Paper Bag Princess* by Robert Munsch
- *Ruby's Rainy Day* by Rosemary Wells
- *Sylvester and the Magic Pebble* by William Steig

Connecting to Imagination: Writing Fiction

- *Abuela* by Arthur Dorros
- *Hey, Al!* by Al Yorinks
- *The Little Engine That Could* by Watty Piper
- *Little Gorilla* by Ruth Bornstein
- *The Paper Bag Princess* by Robert Munsch
- *Ruby's Rainy Day* by Rosemary Wells
- *A Snowy Surprise* by Amy Hest
- *Super Hero* by Marc Tauss
- *Sylvester and the Magic Pebble* by William Steig
- *The Trip* by Ezra Jack Keats

Looking Back, Looking Forward: Making Summer Reading Plans

- *My Kindergarten* by Rosemary Wells

Professional References

Allington, R. (2006). *What really matters for struggling readers: Designing research-based programs*. New York: Pearson.

Allyn, P. (2007). *The complete 4 for literacy*. New York: Scholastic.

Alston, L. (2008). *Why we teach: Learning, laughter, love, and the power to transform lives*. New York: Scholastic.

Anderson, C. (2005). *Assessing writers*. Portsmouth, NH: Heinemann.

Anderson, C. (2000). *How's it going? A practical guide to conferring with student writers*. Portsmouth, NH: Heinemann.

Calkins, L. (1994). *The art of teaching writing*. Portsmouth, NH: Heinemann.

Clay, M. (1991). *Becoming literate: The construction of inner control*. Portsmouth, NH: Heinemann.

Clay, M. (1993). *Reading recovery: A guidebook for teachers in training*. Portsmouth, NH: Heinemann.

Davis-Cole, A. (2004). *When reading begins: The teacher's role in decoding, comprehension, and fluency*. Portsmouth, NH: Heinemann.

Fountas, I. C., & Pinnell, G. S. (2001). *Guiding readers and writers: Teaching comprehension, genre, and content literacy*. Portsmouth, NH: Heinemann.

Fountas, I. C., & Pinnell, G. S. (2000). *Interactive writing: How language and literacy come together, K–2*. Portsmouth, NH: Heinemann.

Fountas, I. C., & Pinnell, G. S. (1999). *Matching books to readers: Using leveled books in guided reading, K–3*. Portsmouth, NH: Heinemann.

Fountas, I. C., & Pinnell, G. S. (1998). *Word matters: Teaching phonics and spelling in the reading/writing classroom*. Portsmouth, NH: Heinemann.

Gentry, J. R. (2008). *Step-by-step assessment guide to code breaking: Pinpoint young students' reading development and provide just-right instruction*. New York: Scholastic.

Goodlad, J. (2004). *A place called school*. New York: McGraw-Hill.

Graves, D. (1989). *Investigate nonfiction*. Portsmouth, NH: Heinemann.

Hahn, M. L. (2002). *Reconsidering read-aloud*. Portland, ME: Stenhouse.

Harvey, S., & Goudvis, A. (2008). *Strategies that work: Teaching comprehension for understanding and engagement, second edition*. Portland, ME: Stenhouse.

Harwayne, S. (2008). *Look who's learning to read: 50 fun ways to instill a love of reading in young children, PreK–K*. New York: Scholastic.

Heard, G. (1999). *Awakening the heart: Exploring poetry in elementary and middle school*. Portsmouth, NH: Heinemann.

Heard, G. (2002). *The revision toolbox: Teaching techniques that work*. Portsmouth, NH: Heinemann.

Henig, R. W. (2003, February 12). Taking play seriously. *The New York Times Magazine*, 40.

Hoyt, L. (2004). *Spotlight on comprehension: Building a literacy of thoughtfulness*. Portsmouth, NH: Heinemann.

Hoyt, L. (2002). *Make it real: Strategies for success with informational text*. Portsmouth, NH: Heinemann.

Hoyt, L. (2008). *Mastering the mechanics, grades K–1: Ready-to-use lessons for modeled, guided, and independent editing*. New York: Scholastic.

Kaufman, D. (2000). *Conferences and conversations: Listening to the literate classroom*. Portsmouth, NH: Heinemann.

Keene, E., & Zimmerman, S. (2007). *Mosaic of thought: The power of comprehension strategy instruction, second edition*. Portsmouth, NH: Heinemann.

Kempton, S. (2007). *The literate kindergarten: Where wonder and discovery thrive*. Portsmouth, NH: Heinemann.

Kovacs, D., & Preller, J. (1993). *Meet the authors and illustrators: 60 creators of favorite children's books talk about their book, vol. 2*. New York: Scholastic.

Krashen, S. (2004). *The power of reading: Insights from the research*. Portsmouth, NH: Heinemann.

Kristo, J., & Bamford, R. (2004). *Nonfiction in focus: A comprehensive framework for helping students become independent readers and writers of nonfiction, K–6.* New York: Scholastic.

Laminack, L. (2007). *Learning under the influence of language and literature: Making the most of read-alouds across the day.* Portsmouth, NH: Heinemann.

Lera, D. (2008). *Writing above standard: Engaging lessons that take standards to new heights and help kids become skilled, inspired writers.* New York: Scholastic.

Miller, D. (2002). *Reading with meaning: Teaching comprehension in the primary grades.* Portland, ME: Stenhouse.

Palmer, R., & Stewart, R. (2003). Nonfiction trade book use in primary grades. *The Reading Teacher, 57*(1), 38–48.

Parkes, B. (2000). *Read it again! Revisiting shared reading.* Portland, ME: Stenhouse.

Pearson, D., & Gallagher, M. (1983). The instruction of reading comprehension. *Contemporary Educational Psychology, 8*(3), 317–345.

Peterson, R., & Eeds, M. (2007). *Grand conversations: Literature groups in action.* New York: Scholastic.

Pinnell, G. S., & Scharer, P. (2003). *Teaching for comprehension in reading, grades K–2.* New York: Scholastic.

Prescott-Griffin, M., & Witherell, N. (2004). *Fluency in focus: Comprehension strategies for all young readers.* Portsmouth, NH: Heinemann.

Rasinski, T. (2003). *The fluent reader: Oral reading strategies for building word recognition.* New York: Scholastic.

Ray, K. W., & Glover, M. *Already ready: Nurturing writers in preschool and kindergarten.* Portsmouth, NH: Heinemann.

Ray, K. W. (1999). *Wondrous words: Writers and writing in the elementary classroom.* Urbana, IL: National Council of Teachers of English.

Rich, M. (2007, November 19). Study links drop in test scores to a decline in time spent reading. *The New York Times,* p.E1, E7.

Robb, L. (2003). *Literacy links: Practical strategies to develop the emergent literacy at-risk children need.* Portsmouth, NH: Heinemann.

Routman, R. (2000). *Kids' poems: Teaching kindergarteners to love writing poetry.* New York: Scholastic.

Routman, R. (2003). *Reading essentials: The specifics you need to teach reading well.* Portsmouth, NH: Heinemann.

Samway, K. D., & Taylor, D. (2007). *Teaching English language learners: Strategies that work.* New York: Scholastic.

Shertzer, M. (1986). *The elements of grammar.* New York: Collier Books.

Silvey, A. (1995). *Children's books and their creators.* Boston: Houghton Mifflin.

Smith, M., & Wilhelm, J. (2007). *Getting it right: Fresh approaches to teaching grammar, usage, and correctness.* New York: Scholastic.

Stead, T. (2006). *Reality checks: Teaching reading comprehension with nonfiction, K–5.* Portland, ME: Stenhouse.

Strunk, W., & White, E. B. (1999). *The elements of style* (4th ed.) New York: Longman.

Sulzby, E. (1991). Assessment of emergent literacy: Storybook reading. *The Reading Teacher, 44*(7), 498–500.

Szymusiak, K., & Sibberson, F. (2001). *Beyond leveled books: Supporting transitional readers in grades 2–5.* Portland, ME: Stenhouse.

Welty, E. (1984). *One writer's beginnings.* Cambridge, MA: Harvard University.